THE LIFE OF ST. ANSGAR

St. Rimbert of Hamburg

Introduction by: D.P. Curtin
Translation by: Charles H. Robinson

THE LIFE OF ST. ANSGAR

Copyright @ 2008 Dalcassian Publishing Company

All rights reserved. No part of this publication may be reproduced, distributed, or transmitted in any form or by any means, including photocopying, recording, or other electronic or mechanical methods, without the prior written permission of the publisher, except in the case of brief quotations embodied in critical reviews and certain other non-commercial uses permitted by copyright law. For permission request, write to Dalcassian Publishing Company at dalcassianpublishing at gmail.com

ISBN: 979-8-8693-3086-4 (Paperback)

Library of Congress Control Number:
Author: Curtin, D.P. (1985-)

Printed by Ingram Content Group, 1 Ingram Blvd, La Vergne, Tennessee

First printing edition 2008.

INTRODUCTION

Today, little is remembered about the illustrious St. Ansgar, Archbishop of Hamburg and great Apostle of the North. Even amongst Germano-Nordic Catholic circles his name has been obscured by the passing of centuries, a relic of an ancient order that might be observed in passing in some old stained-glass window, but not a figure of living historical memory. Perhaps this is the fate of all mankind. Those figures which we consider to be pivotal today, politicians, celebrities, and their ilk, tomorrow will be obscure artifacts collecting dust in the pages of a book or in a museum, forgotten by all except a select few who seek out the arcane. Such an observation should make us submit humbly to the unstoppable force of time, and the recognition of the little place that we occupy in God's mysterious order for the world.

St. Ansgar was a man who, in his own lifetime, guided the course of European history through his mission on the fringes of the Carolingian Empire. In the early 9th century Scandinavia was still a largely unknown land, charted by some cartographers but beyond the vista of civilization. Legends abounded regarding the people who inhabited these lands, most of which framed them as barbaric and semi-cannibalistic. The force of sovereignty and law had yet to be planted in the far north, and there was an abiding fear of the tribes that resided there. St. Ansgar was called to the still ferocious and pagan lands of Sweden by the request of Bjorn II in 829, laying the foundation for the church there, an institution that is still active to this day. His establishment of the Swedish church was done without an episcopal appointment, and he remained within the jurisdiction of the Frankish bishops who oversaw his work. Directly following this, he was called by the Emperor Louis I the Pious and granted an appointment as the Archbishop of Hamburg, then as now a significant North Sea port city. This appointment, while perhaps an improvement from his post in hostile rural Sweden, was still a substantial political trial for the churchman. Viking raids were at their apex at this time, and the local Saxon population, recently converted to Christianity, was ambivalent to the episcopal see in Hamburg. One Danish expedition in 845 outright demolished the ecclesiastical library established in the town, threatening to diminish the light of learning in the North. This raid by the Danes remains as a sentinel event in the history of the city and is still commemorated to this day.

Through his connections to both the Imperial Frankish court and the various petty Danish kings, such as Horik I the Elder, Ansgar was able to create endowments for his missionary works and gain the gradual approval of the local Saxon and Danish populations. Practically, his efforts introduced the art of the written word to the North; established schools that would lay the foundation of centralized royal courts; and created international diplomacy that would firmly plant the idea of statehood in the early Scandinavian nations. Spiritually, Christian morality created a sense of moral restraint to the populace and granted them the ability to organize themselves for social activities other than military combat, tribal contests of brute strength, and the endless parade of cattle raids. Moreover, the imparting of the Christian Gospel granted these people of the North a new dignity, recognizing that they were children of the same God as their southern counterparts and, by extension, equal to them in the sight of God. The unbridled warrior machismo of the pagan past had no such egality. Kings and their warriors succeeded by the will of the gods because of their innate divine superiority and were therefore worthy of accolades because of their ephemeral political triumph. Ansgar's efforts forged in-roads to the Danish court and continued under his successor St. Rimbert (also the author of this text). This in time resulted in the conversion of Denmark in 965, under Harald Bluetooth, and the establishment of the Church of Denmark, the polity of which survives (in Lutheran form) to this day.

The patience and personal fortitude necessary to observe the Christian Gospel in the face of such unrestrained hostility remains a message for our own time, particularly as the West slinks back into the mire of a new dark age, one made all the more protracted by the pantheon of secular idols. In attempting to confront the savage undercurrent of politicians, the litany of our modern paganism, and the human cruelty which so often wears ideological drag, we might best look to the past, to others who have come this way before, and take a bit of wisdom from their suffering and lived experience. For St. Ansgar, the art of confronting the barbarity of his own age with an act of abiding love is what makes him worthy of memory and emulation, and why his story remains relevant to us some twelve centuries later. Perhaps, in some future epoch, the historical Ansgar will totally fade from our collective memory, and we will have forgotten all the dealings of this saint, but the light of faith and the love of God which he inspired among the people of the north will remain with us, so long as we actively attend to it.

D.P. Curtin
F&M College
Lancaster, PA

THE LIFE OF ST. ANSGAR

CHAPTER I.

The sons and disciples of the most reverend Father Ansgar, to whom has been granted everlasting happiness, salute the holy fathers and brethren who are God's soldiers in the sacred monastery of Corbey to whom special veneration and affection in the love of Christ are due, and they pray for the peace and safety of those who rule over them in the Lord.

Having enjoyed for a long time, through God's favour, the services of their good pastor, and having been instructed by his preaching and example and supported by his merits and intercessions, we, who have now been deprived of his presence, have carefully considered how far we ought to grieve on our own account and how far we ought to give thanks on his behalf. For the true worshipper of God, who abstains from every evil deed and continues simple and unassuming, creates in others the assurance that when he is taken away, he will speedily reach Him whom he has loved with utmost devotion and to whom his thoughts have ever been directed. For this reason, we believe that we ought indeed to give thanks for the recompense that has been granted to him; whilst, in view of our own loss, we must need pray that we who, as men, have been deprived of so great a pastor, may be found worthy to receive divine help from heaven. Amid the difficult circumstances in which we are placed we rightly perceive what we have lost and understand what reason we have to grieve on our own behalf. Whilst he was still alive it seemed as though we lacked nothing, for in him we rejoiced to possess everything. For kings respected his holiness, the pastors of the churches venerated him, the clergy imitated him, and all the people admired him. And whilst all men declared him to be holy and upright, we, as the body of which lie was the head, were respected and praised on account of his goodness. Now that we are deprived of so great a benefit we dare not have regard to our own merits, but we fear rather lest, as a result of our sins, we should be exposed to the teeth of wolves : for the world, which lieth in evil, seeks to overthrow that which is just and holy, rather than to build tip that which is deserving of veneration. And the devil, who is the enemy of the human race, when lie sees that anyone is leading an especially devout and religious life, endeavors the more to create obstacles so that lie may destroy what is holy, and may by crafty persuasion and wicked endeavor take it away so that it be not imitated by others. As then we sigh amidst these perils, and for the time being are in fear of manifold evils, we know that we must seek the help of God whose compassion will not, we believe, fail despite our unworthiness. Accordingly with suppliant hearts we beseech and implore your holiness that you will remember and deign to intercede before God on our behalf that His compassion fail us not, but that, as our most kind lielper, He may drive all evil away from us, and be to us a refuge in tribulation, and that He may not desert those who hope in Him. Presuming then on His mercy and placing all our hope in His compassion, we leave to His discretion what we ought to obtain for ourselves and how we ought hereafter to live, and with our whole heart and mind we praise and glorify His grace for that He granted us to enjoy for a time such a patron. We render great thanks to your most reverend paternity and holiness that by your kindness and consent we have been thought worthy to have such a father. If anyone should desire to imitate his example lie will enjoy, while upon earth, the society of heaven; if any shall recall his teaching, he will be able to walk without failing in the way of God's commandments; if any shall listen to his exhortations, he will take pains to guard against the snares of the enemy.

We have decided to write down the mernorials of this most holy father and to make known to you how he lived with us and what we know concerning him, in order that you may, with us, praise the divine mercy that was manifested in this blessed man and that his sacred devotion inay show the way of salvation to those who are willing to imitate him.

CHAPTER II.

His sanctity and piety tended to increase from his earliest youth and at each stage in his life he tended to increase in holiness. For in his infancy be received from heaven spiritual revelations, and by the grace of the Lord be frequently received celestial visits which admonished him to turn away his thoughts from things on earth and to keep his whole heart open to heavenly influences.

He had made known these revelations to certain of us who were closely associated with him on condition that they were declared to no one during his lifetime. Now that he is dead, we have decided to insert these revelations in this work for the praise of God, that those who read may know with what great grace the Lord deigned to train his servant from his earliest age, and afterwards to render him illustrious by means of his meritorious actions. He used to relate that when he was a boy about five years old, his mother, who feared God and was very religious, died, and that soon afterward his father sent him to schoolto learn his letters. When he had taken his place he began, as boys of that age are wont to do, to act in a childish way with the boys of his own age, and to give attention to foolish talk and jests rather than to learning. When he had thus given himself up to boyish levity, he had a vision during the night in which he appeared to be in a miry and slippery place, from which be could not escape except with great difficulty ; beside him was a delightful path on which he saw a matron advancing, who was distinguished by her beauty and nobility, and was followed by many other women clothed in white, with whom was his mother. When he recognized her, he wished to run to her, but he could not easily emerge from that miry and slippery place. When the women drew near to him, the one who appeared to be the mistress of the rest and whom lie confidently believed to be the Holy Mary, said to him : " My son, do you wish to come to your mother? and when he replied that he eagerly desired to do so she answered : " If you desire to share our companionship, you must flee from every kind of vanity, and put away childish jests and have regard to the seriousness of life ; for we hate everything that is vain and unprofitable, nor can anyone be with us who has delight in such things." Immediately after this vision be began to be serious and to avoid childish associations, and to devote himself more constantly to reading and meditation and other useful occupations, so that his companions marveled greatly that his manner of life had so suddenly changed.

CHAPTER III.

When later on he received from you the tonsure and had begun to grow up under monastic teaching human weakness came upon him and the strength of his early resolve began to weaken. Meanwhile he happened to hear of the death of the most excellent Emperor Charles [i.e. Charlemagne who died January 28th, 814, aged 71] whom he had before seen in power and honor, and who, as he had heard, had governed the kingdom in a praiseworthy manner and with great prudence. The death of so great an emperor affected him with fear and horror, and he began to return to his former state of mind and to recall the words of admonition uttered by the holy Mother of God.

Accordingly, he put aside all levity and began to languish with a divinely inspired remorse; and, devoting himself wholly to the service of God, he gave attention to prayer, watching and fasting. By these virtuous exercises he became a true athlete, of God, and, as a result of his persistent severity, the world became dead to him and he to the world. [Cf. Gal vi.14]

When the Day of Pentecost came, the grace of the Holy Spirit, which was at this time poured forth upon the apostles, enlightened and refreshed his mind so we believe ; and the same night lie saw in a vision that he was about to encounter sudden death when, in the very act of dying, he summoned to his aid the holy apostle Peter and the blessed John the Baptist. When, as it seemed to him, his soul was in the act of leaving his body and was taking to itself another and very beautiful kind of body which was no longer subject to death, and from which all disquiet was absent, at the very moment of his death and of wondering surprise these two men appeared. The elder of the two he recognized at once, without being told, by his white head, his straight and thick locks, his ruddy face, his sad countenance, his white and colored dress, and his short stature, as St. Peter. The other was a youth taller of stature, with flowing beard, brown and curly hair, lean face, and cheerful countenance, and was dressed in a silken robe. Him he knew to be St. John. These, then, stood on either side of him, and as his soul left his body lie seemed to be surrounded by an unending light which filled the whole world. By means of this light and without any effort on his part, the saints mentioned above led him in a strange and indescribable way till they came to a certain place which, without making any enquiry, he knew to be the fire of purgatory, and here they left him. When he had suffered much and seemed to have experienced the blackest darkness and the most enormous pressure and choking, he was deprived of all memory and his only thought was how could so terrible a punishment exist. When he had been tortured here for three days, as he thought though the time seemed to him to be more than a thousand years, because of the greatness of the suffering - the men before mentioned returned and stood by him with much greater joy than before. Advancing with a yet more delightful progress they led him through great and ineffable brightness, progressing without motion and by no material path. To adopt his own words: " I saw," he said, " from afar, various ranks of saints, some nearer to me and some standing far from the east, but looking towards it, and together praising Him who appeared in the east, whilst some worshipped with bent heads, downcast faces and outstretched hands. When we had arrived at the place where the light rises, we beheld four-and-twenty elders, even as it is written in the Apocalypse, who appeared sitting in their seats whilst leaving abundant room for others to approach. They also looked with reverence towards the east and offered to God unspeakable praises. The praises of those who sang all together brought to me the most delightful refreshment, but after I returned to my body I could by no means retain them in my mind. In the east, where the light rises, was a marvelous brightness, an unapproachable light of unlimited and excessive brilliance, in which was included every splendid colour and everything delightful to the eye. All the ranks of the saints, who stood round rejoicing, derived their happiness therefrom. The brightness was of such a great extent that I could see neither beginning nor end thereof.

When I was able to look round both far and near amidst the unending light, I could not see what was within, but saw only, the outside edge; nevertheless, I believed that He was there concerning whom Peter said, " on whom the angels desire to look." [I Peter i, 12]

From Him proceeded unlimited brightness whereby the saints far and near were illuminated. He too was, in a sense, in all of them, and they in Him. He surrounded everything from outside; He controlled and met the needs of all; He protected them from above and sustained them from beneath. The sun and the moon afforded no light there; neither was the earth nor the firmament visible. But even this brightness was not such as to interfere with the sight of those who gazed, but it was at once most pleasing to the eyes and brought complete satisfaction to the mind. When I spoke of the elders sitting I meant that in a certain sense they may be said to have sat. For there was nothing material there, nothing possessed anybody, although there was an appearance as of a body which I cannot describe. The beautiful light round those who were sitting proceeded from (God) Himself and extended like a rainbow. When, then I had been brought by the men whom I mentioned into the presence of this unending light, where the majesty of Almighty God was revealed to me without need for anyone to explain, and when they and I had offered our united adoration, a most sweet voice, the sound of which was more distinct than all other sounds, and which seemed to me to fill the whole world, came forth from the same divine majesty, and addressed me and said, "Go and return to Me crowned with martyrdom." At the sound of this voice the whole choir of saints who were praising God became silent and adored with downcast faces. I saw throughout no form from which these words, proceeded, After hearing the voice I become sad, because I was compelled to return to the earth; but, satisfied with the promise that I should return, I turned to depart with the beforementioned leaders. As they came and returned with me they spoke not a word, but they looked on me with pious affection even as a mother looks upon her only son. Thus, it was that 1 returned to the body. In going and returning I experienced no difficulty or delay, because we arrived at once at the place to which we went. Though I seem to have told something of the greatest of all delights, I confess that the pen can in no way express all of which the mind is conscious. Nor is the mind conscious of what actually existed, for that was revealed to me which eye has not seen, nor car heard, nor has entered into the heart of man." [I Cor ii, 9]

As a result of this vision, which I have described in the words which he had himself dictated, the servant of God was both terrified and comforted, and in the fear of the Lord lie began to live more carefully, to cleave day by day to good deeds, and to hope that by the mercy of God, in whatever way He might choose, he might be able to obtain the crown of martyrdom. [Cf. Chap XL and XLII]

Though the threatening sword did not bring about the martyrdom of his body, we shall more fully explain, when we conic to speak of his death, how this promise was, by God's mercy, fulfilled by his death upon the cross which lie ever bore about in his body for the honor of Christ's name.

CHAPTER IV.

Later on, when he had become the master of the school dedicated to St. Peter, as he went and returned to its door it was his custom to pray earnestly and in secret in the oratory of St. John the Baptist. Two years after the vision mentioned above, he had a vision in the night in which he thought that he had turned into the oratory in order to pray, and when he had risen from prayer a man came through the door who was tall, dressed according to Jewish custom, and of handsome appearance. From his eyes a divine lustre radiated like unto a flame of fire. When he beheld Him he cast aside all hesitancy and, believing that it was the Lord Christ, lie ran forward and fell at His feet. As he lay prostrate on his face, He (the Lord Christ) commanded him to rise. When lie had risen and was standing reverently before Him he could not gaze upon His face for the glorious light that flashed from His eyes. With a soothing voice He addressed him and said: " Declare thine iniquities in order that thou mayest be justified," to Whom God's servant replied, "Lord, why must I tell Thee? Thou knowest all and nothing is hid from Thee." He replied again: " I know all, but I will that men should confess their faults to Me in order that they may receive forgiveness." When he had declared to Him everything that he had done since his earliest youth, and had then prostrated himself in prayer, He (the Christ) stood erect before him and said: " Fear not, for I am He that blotteth out thy iniquities," after which saying, the figure whom he had seen in his vision retired. The man of God rose from his sleep, and, strengthened by the assurance that his sins had been forgiven, rejoiced with exceeding joy.

CHAPTER V.

It happened at this time, as you well know, that a certain youth in the school named Fulbert, was struck by one of his companions with a piece of wood, and was brought to the point of death. The before-mentioned servant of God was greatly distressed at this, because such carelessness had occurred amongst those under his control and whilst he was acting as master. When the hour of the boy's death drew High lie was lying on a couch, overcome by sleep, when he saw in a dream the boy's soul withdrawn from his body and carried by angel ministers to heaven, and in a strange and indescribable way he was allowed by God to accompany the boy's soul. When they had passed into heaven he saw the soul of the boy taken into a shining dwelling and placed amongst the ranks of the martyrs. He was moreover given to understand that, inasmuch as the boy had borne the wound inflicted upon him with patience, and had loved his brother's soul even unto death, and had prayed earnestly on behalf of his assailant, his patience and goodness had been rewarded by God, and he had been placed amongst the martyr bands.

This revelation was made to him so quickly at the hour of the boy's death that while lie was still waiting the venerable father Witmar who at that time shared with him the superintendence of the school, and was present and witnessed this occurrence, roused him and told him of the death of his pupil, whereupon he answered that lie already knew of it. The Lord's grace permitted him to see this vision in order that he might be consoled and in order that, in view of his exceeding sorrow, the boy's salvation might lighten his distress.

CHAPTER VI.

By these and many other revelations and visions the man of God was divinely strengthened, and of the increase of his sanctity and goodness you have still better proof provided by eyewitnesses. We, who desire to tell of what has happened in our midst, [Cf. Chap I, note] must first enquire for the benefit of those who may chance to be ignorant, how he came to leave his secured position and by what impulse and force of circumstances, after dedicating himself to God in your presence and promising to render obedience, he came to these parts and was raised to the office of a bishop in our midst. We have thought that it was necessary to write this for fear lest anyone should attribute to fickleness the task which the man of God undertook for the saving of souls, moved by divine compassion and by a desire to go to foreign parts There was built in former times in this part of Saxony the monastery which was first founded by your authority and direction [I.e. under the direction of the aboot Adelard] and, having by God's help been completed at a later time, was called New Corbey, the name having been adapted from your own dwelling place. To this place then, God's servant was first sent in company with other brethren in order that he might perform the office of a teacher. In this task he was found so commendable and agreeable that, by the choice of all, he was appointed to preach the word of God to the people in church. So it came about that in this same place he became the first master of the school and teacher of the people.

CHAPTER VII.

After this it happened that a king named Harald, who ruled over some of the Danes, was assailed by hatred and malignity, and was driven from his kingdom by the other kings of the same province.

He came to his serene majesty the emperor Ludovic [ie. Ludwig] and asked that be might be thought worthy to receive his help so that he might be able to regain his kingdom. While the emperor kept him at his court he urged him, by personal persuasion and through the instrumentality of others, to accept the Christian faith, because there would then be a more intimate friendship between them, and a Christian people would more readily come to his aid and to the aid of his friends if both peoples were worshippers of the same God. At length, by the assistance of divine grace, he brought about his conversion, and when lie bad been sprinkled with the holy water of baptism he himself received him from the sacred font and adopted him as his son. When, then, he desired to send him back to his own land in order that he might, by his assistance, seek to recover his dominions, he began to make diligent enquiry in order that he might find a holy and devoted man who could go and continue with him, and who might strengthen him and his people, and by teaching the doctrine of salvation might induce them to receive the faith of the Lord. At a public gathering of his chief men, at which their priests and other good men were present, the emperor referred to this matter and earnestly begged all of them to find someone who would volunteer for this difficult and honorable task. When they refused and said that they knew of no one who was possessed of so great devotion as to be willing to undertake this dangerous journey for the name of Christ, Wala, who was at that time the much respected abbot of our monastery, stood forth and said to the emperor that he knew a monk in his monastery who burned with zeal for true religion and was eager to endure suffering for the name of God. He declared, however, that he did not know whether lie would be willing to undertake this journey. Why say more? At the king's command Ansgar was summoned to the palace, and the abbot explained to him everything that had been done and told the reason for his being summoned. He replied that as an obedient monk he was ready to serve God in all things that were commanded him. He was then brought into the presence of the emperor, who asked him whether on God's behalf and for the sake of preaching the gospel amongst the Danish peoples, he would become the companion of Harald, whereupon he replied that he was entirely willing. When the abbot had further stated that lie would by no means impose this upon him as a command, but if of his own free will he chose to do it he would be pleased and would give him his authoritative consent, he replied that he none the less chose the task and desired by all means to carry it through. When at length this was publicly announced, and it became known to all who lived in the abbot's house, many began to express astonishment at his strength of purpose and his willingness to abandon his country and his acquaintances and the love of the brethren with whom he had been brought up, and to visit foreign nations and hold intercourse with unknown and barbarous peoples. Many also deprecated his action, and assailed him with reproaches, whilst some endeavored to divert him from his purpose, but the man of God continued steadfast in his resolve. When the abbot went, day by day, to the palace, he remained at home and avoided the society of all men and, choosing for himself a lonely spot in a neighboring vineyard, he devoted his time to prayer and to reading. There was at that time with the abbot a certain brother belonging to our monastery named Autbertus. When Autbertus saw that he was anxious and distressed and that each day he kept himself apart and did not associate or speak with anyone, he began to feet pity for him, and on a certain day he went to the place where lie was sitting by himself in the vineyard and asked him whether he really desired to undertake this journey. Ansgar, who hoped that this enquiry was not prompted by compassion, but was made with some further object, replied : " Why is this a matter of concern to you ? Do not disturb me by making such an enquiry." He declared that he was making. No pretense, but that he really desired to know whether he proposed to continue in the purpose which he had formed. Then Ansgar thanked him for his kindness, and said, " I am asked whether I am willing on God's behalf to go to pagan nations in order to preach the gospel. So far from daring to oppose this suggestion I desire, with all my strength, that the opportunity for going may be granted to me, and that no one may be able to divert me from this design."

Then the brother beforementioned said to him I will never suffer you to go alone, but I desire, for the love of God, to go with you, provided only that you can obtain the consent of the lord abbot." When then, they had ratified their agreement, Ansgar presented himself to the abbot on his return to the monastery, and explained to him that he had found a companion who, of his own free will, desired to share his journey. When the abbot asked who it was, and he mentioned the brother Autbertus, he was greatly astonished, as he had never imagined that he, who belonged to a noble family and was his intimate friend and was regarded as the chief administrator of the monastery after himself, would be willing to undertake such a task. Nevertheless, he summoned him and questioned him concerning the matter. He replied that he could not bear that Ansgar should go alone, but that for the name of Christ he desired to become his comforter and helper, should he obtain the consent of the abbot and of the brethren. The abbot replied that he would give his consent if of his own free will he chose to undertake this journey, but that he would not depute anyone in his house to act as a servant unless he could be induced to go voluntarily.

The venerable abbot did not act thus through any lack of regard for Ansgar, but because at that time it seemed to him to be abhorrent and wrong that anyone should be compelled against his will to live amongst pagans. The two monks were subsequently brought before the king, who was gratified by their willingness and desire to undertake this task, and who gave them whatever was necessary for the performance of their ministerial functions, also writing cases, tents and other things that would be helpful and which seemed likely to be needed on their great journey. He bade them go with Harald and commanded them to devote the utmost care to his profession of faith and by their godly exhortations to confirm in the faith both Harald and his companions who had been baptized together with him, for fear lest at the instigation of the devil they should return to their former errors, and at the same time by their preaching to urge others to accept the Christian religion. Having been then dismissed by the emperor they had none to render them any menial service, as no one in the abbot's household would go with them of his own accord, and he would compel no one to go against his will. Harald, to whom they had been committed, was as yet ignorant and untaught in the faith, and was unaware how God's servants ought to behave. Moreover, his companions who had been recently converted and had been trained in a very different faith, paid them little attention. Having started then with considerable difficulty they arrived at Cologne. At that time there was a venerable bishop there named Hadebald. He had compassion upon their needs and presented them with a good boat in which they might place their possessions and in which there were two cabins which had been suitably prepared for them. When Harald saw the boat, he decided to remain with them in it, so that he and they could each have a cabin. This tended to promote an increase of friendship and goodwill between them; his companions also, from this time forward, paid careful attention to their wants.

On leaving the boat they passed through Dorstadt [I.e. Wijk te Duerstade, near Utrecht. Willibrord and Boniface had both preached there] and crossing the neighboring territory of the Frisians came to the Danish borders. As King Harald could not for the time being obtain peaceful possession of his kingdom, the emperor gave him a place beyond the River Elbe so that if it were necessary he might halt there.

THE LIFE OF ST. ANSGAR

CHAPTER VIIII.

Accordingly the servants of God, who were with him, and who were stationed at one time amongst Christians and at other times amongst pagans, began to apply themselves to the word of God ; and those whom they could influence they directed into the way of truth, so that many were converted to the faith by their example and teaching, and the number of those who should be saved in the Lord increased daily. They themselves, being inspired by divine love, in order to spread their holy religion, made diligent search for boys whom they might endeavor to educate for the service of God. Harald also gave some of his own. household to be educated by them; and so it came about that in a short time they established a school for twelve or more boys. [For site of this school see Chap XXIV] Others they took as servants or helpers, and their reputation and the religion which they preached in God's name were spread abroad. After they, had spent two years or more in this good work brother Autbertus became grievously afflicted with illness, and on this account he was carried to New Corbey where, as his weakness increased day by day, at Easter time even as it had been before revealed to him by the Lord he ended his life, passing away happily, as we believe.

CHAPTER IX.

Meanwhile [I.e. in 829] it happened that Swedish ambassadors had come to the Emperor Ludovic, and, amongst other matters which they had been ordered to bring to the attention of the emperor, they informed him that there were many belonging to their nation who desired to embrace the Christian religion, and that their king so far favored this suggestion that lie would permit God's priests to reside there, provided that they might be deemed worthy of such a favor and that the emperor would send them suitable preachers. When the Godfearing emperor heard this lie was greatly delighted, and a second time he endeavored to find men whom he might send to those districts, who might discover whether this people was prepared to accept the faith, as tile ambassadors had assured him, and might begin to inculcate the observance of the Christian religion. So, it came about that his serene majesty began once again to discuss the matter with your abbot and asked him whether by chance lie could find one of his monks who, for the name of Christ, was willing to go into those parts; or who would go and stay with Harald while God's servant Ansgar, who was with him, undertook this mission. Thus, it was that Ansgar was summoned by royal command to the palace and was told that he should not even stop to shave himself before coining into the royal presence. The man of God, who knew clearly beforehand for what purpose he was being summoned, burned with fervor and with love towards God and esteemed it a special joy if he might be allowed to press forward in the work of winning souls for Flim. If in a journey of this kind any harm or misfortune should befall him, he was resolved to bear it patiently for Christ's sake; and he had no hesitation in undertaking this task, as he was comforted by the heavenly vision which he had previously seen. At the time to which we refer, when lie was staying with you and had already been divinely enlightened by two visions [Cf. Chap II and IV] it seemed to him one night that he had come to a house in which were standing many preachers who had been prepared for their task of preaching. In their presence he was suddenly transported, and he saw shining around him a light from heaven which excelled the brightness of the sun; and, as he marveled what this might be, a voice like unto that which he declared that he had heard in his first vision said to him : "Thy sin is forgiven." In answer to which voice, being, as we believe, divinely inspired, he said: "Lord, what wilt thou have me to do? " Again, the voice was heard saying: " Go, and declare the word of God unto the nations." As God's servant thought upon this vision he rejoiced in the Lord greatly, for he perceived that what had been commanded him was in part accomplished, and desired to add to his labors by preaching the word of God to the Swedes. When then, he was brought into the presence of the emperor and was asked by him whether he was willing to undertake this mission, he replied readily that he was prepared to undertake any task which the emperor might decide to place upon him for the name of Christ.

CHAPTER X.

In the good providence of God, the venerable abbot [I.e Wala] found for him amongst your fraternity a companion, namely the prior Witmar, who was both worthy and willing to undertake this great task. He further arranged that the good father Gislemar, a man approved by faith and good works, and by his fervent zeal for God, should be with Harald. Ansgar then undertook the mission committed to him by the emperor, who desired that he should go to the Swedes and discover whether these people were prepared to accept the faith as their messengers had declared. How great and serious were the calamities which lit; suffered while engaged in this mission, father Witmar, who himself shared them, can best tell. It may suffice for me to say that while they were in the midst of their journey they fell into the hands of pirates. The merchants with whom they were travelling, defended themselves vigorously and for a time successfully, but eventually they were conquered and overcome by the pirates, who took from them their ships and all that they possessed, whilst they themselves barely escaped on. foot to land. They lost here the royal gifts which they should have delivered there, together with all their other possessions, save only what they were able to take and carry with them as they left the ship. They were plundered, moreover, of nearly forty books which they had accumulated for the service of God. When this happened, some were disposed to turn and go back, but no argument could divert God's servant from the journey which he had undertaken. On the contrary, he submitted everything that might happen to him to God's will, and was by no means disposed to return till, by God's help, he could ascertain whether he would be allowed to preach the gospel in those parts.

CHAPTER XI.

With great difficulty they accomplished their long journey on foot, traversing also the intervening seas, where it was possible, by ship, and eventually arrived at the Swedish port called Birka.

They were kindly received here by the king, who was called Biörn, whose messengers had informed him of the reason for which they had come. When he understood the object of their mission, and had discussed the matter with his friends, with the approval and consent of all have granted them permission to remain there and to preach the gospel of Christ, and offered liberty to any who desired it to accept their teaching. Accordingly, the servants of God, when they saw that matters had turned out propitiously as they had desired, began eagerly to preach the word of salvation to the people of that place. There were many who were well disposed towards their mission and who willingly listened to the teaching of the Lord. There were also many Christians who were held captive amongst them, and who rejoiced that now at last they were able to participate in the divine mysteries. It was thus made clear that everything was as their messengers had declared to the emperor, and some of them desired earnestly to receive the grace of baptism. These included the prefect of this town named Herigar, who was a counsellor of the king and much beloved by him. He received the gift of holy baptism and was strengthened in the Catholic faith. A little later he built a church on his own ancestral property and served God with the utmost devotion. Several remarkable deeds were accomplished by the man who afforded many proofs of his invincible faith, as we shall make clear in the following narrative.

CHAPTER XII.

When the servants of God had spent another half year [I.e. altogether a year and a half] with them and had attained the object of their mission they returned to the emperor and took with them letters written by the king himself in characters fashioned after the Swedish custom. They were received with great honour and goodwill by the emperor, to whom they narrated all that the Lord had wrought by them, and how in those parts the door of faith was opened by which these nations were bidden to enter. When the most pious emperor heard this, he rejoiced greatly and as he recalled the beginning which had been made in establishing the worship of God amongst the Danes, he rendered praise and thanks to Almighty God, and, being inflamed with zeal for the faith, he began to enquire by what means lie might establish a bishop's see in the north within the limits of his own empire, from which the bishop who should be stationed there might make frequent journeys to the northern regions for the sake of preaching the gospel, and from which all these barbarous nations might easily and profitably receive the sacraments of the divine mystery. As he was pursuing this matter with anxious care he learnt, from information provided by some of his trusty companions, that when his father, the Emperor Charles, of glorious memory, had subdued the whole of Saxony by the sword and had subjected it to the yoke of Christ, he divided it into dioceses, but did not commit to any bishop the furthest part of this province which lay beyond the river Elbe, but decided that it should be reserved in order that he might establish there an archiepiscopal see from which, with the Lord's help, the Christian faith might successively spread to the nations that lay beyond. He, accordingly, caused the first church that was built there to be consecrated by a Gallic bishop named Amalliar. Later on he specially committed the care of this parish to a priest named Heridac, [Or Heridag] as he did not wish that the neighbouring bishops should have any authority over this place. He had further arranged to have this priest consecrated as a bishop, but his speedy departure from this life [lit. from this light] prevented this being done. After the death of this much-tobe-remembered emperor his son Ludovic, who was placed on his father's throne, acting on the suggestion of others, divided in two that part of the province which lies beyond the river Elbe and entrusted it, for the time being, to two neighbouring bishops [I.e. The bishops of Verden and Bremen] for he paid no attention to the arrangement which his father had made in regard to this matter, or, possibly, he was altogether ignorant of it. When the time came that the faith of Christ began, by God's grace, to bear fruit in the lands of the Danes and Swedes, and his father's wish became known to him, he was unwilling that this wish should remain unaccomplished and, acting with the approval of the bishops and a largely attended synod, he established an archiepiscopal see in the town of Hamburg, which is situated in the farthest part of Saxony beyond the river Elbe. He desired that the whole Church of the Nordalbingi should be subject to this archbishopric, and that it should possess the power of appointing bishops and priests who for the name of Christ might go out into these districts.

To this see, therefore, the emperor caused the holy Ansgar, our lord and father, to be consecrated as archbishop by the hands of Drogo, Bishop of Metz, and at that time principal chaplain at the imperial court. He was assisted by Ebo, Archbishop of Rheims; Hetti of Trier [Hetti, or Hetto, was archbishop of Trier, 814-847] and Otgar of Mainz [Otgar was bishop of Mainz 826-847], whilst many other bishops who had gathered for the imperial assembly were present. The bishops Helmgaud [Bishop of Verden] and

Willerick, from whom Ansgar took over the abovementioned parts of this ecclesiastical district, approved and took part in his consecration.

Inasmuch as this diocese was situated in dangerous regions, and it was to be feared that it might come to an end in consequence of the savagery of the barbarians by which it was threatened, and because its area was small, the emperor handed over to his representatives a monastery in Gaul, called Turholt, to be always at its service.

CHAPTER XIII.

In order that these arrangements should be permanently established the emperor sent Ansgar to the apostolic see, and by his messengers the venerable bishops Bernold [Bishop of Strassburg] and Ratold [Bishop of Verona, ob. 874.] and the illustrious count Gerold, he caused the whole matter to be made known to Pope Gregory [I.e. Gregory IV, 827-844] so that it might receive his confirmation. The Pope confirmed this, not only by an authoritative decree, but also by the gift of the pallium, in accordance with the custom of his predecessors, and he appointed him as his legate for the time being amongst all the neighbouring races of the Swedes and Danes, also the Slavs and the other races that inhabited the regions of the north, so that he might share authority with Ebo the Archbishop of Rheims, to whom he had before entrusted the same office. At the tomb of the holy apostle Peter he publicly committed to him authority to evangelize these races. And, for fear lest anything that he had done should prove ineffectual in time to come, he smote with his curse any who should resist, or contradict, or in any way attempt to interfere with the holy intentions of the emperor and committed such an one to everlasting vengeance and the companionship of devils.

As we have already said, the same office of legate had before been entrusted by Pope Paschal {Paschal I 817-824] to Ebo, the Archbishop of Rheims. Ebo himself, inspired by the Spirit of God, burned with eager desire to draw to the Christian fold the non-Christian races and specially the Danes whom lie had often seen at the palace and who, as he grieved to see, had been led astray by the wiles of the devil. In order to promote their salvation he longed to sacrifice himself and all that be possessed. The emperor had given him a place situated beyond the river Elbe, which was called Welanao, so that whenever he went into those parts he might have a place in which to stay. Accordingly he frequently went to this place and distributed much money in the northern districts in order that he might win the souls of the people; and he attached many to the Christian religion and strengthened them in the catholic faith.

CHAPTER XIV.

After the consecration of the holy Ansgar our lord and father, those who shared the office of legate, conferred together, and decided that it was necessary that an assistant bishop should be consecrated who might exercise the episcopal office amongst the Swedes, inasmuch as the chief bishop could not be expected to be present so far away, and Ansgar himself could not be in both places. With the consent then, and approval of the emperor, the venerable Ebo sent to Sweden a relation of his own named Gautbert who had been chosen for this work and had been given the honorable rank of a bishop He supplied him in abundance with all that was wanted for his ecclesiastical office and for his necessary expenditure at his own cost and that of the emperor. Having himself undertaken, by apostolic authority, the office of an evangelist, he appointed Gautbert to act as legate on his behalf amongst the Swedes. To him, too, the emperor, at the suggestion of the same bishop Ebo, gave the monastery which he had himself built at Welanao, to serve as a place of refuge, in order that the performance of his task might be rendered permanent and secure. This Gautbert, who at his consecration received the honored name of the apostle Simeon, went to Sweden, and was honorably received by the king [I.e. King Biorn, cf. Chap xi.] and the people; and he began, amidst general goodwill and approval, to build a church there and to preach the faith of the gospel, and there was great rejoicing amongst the Christians who were living there, and the number of those who believed increased daily.

CHAPTER XV.

Meanwhile our lord and master diligently executed his office in the diocese that had been committed to him, and in the country of the Danes, and by the example of his good life he incited many to embrace the faith. He began also to buy Danish and Slav boys and to redeem some from captivity so that he might train them for God's service. Of these he kept some with him, whilst others he sent to be trained at the monastery of Turholt. There were also with him here belonging to your order some of our fathers and teachers, as a result of whose teaching and instructions the divine religion has increased amongst us.

CHAPTER XVI.

While these events, which brought praise and honor to God, were taking place in both directions, pirates suddenly arrived and surrounded the town of Hamburg. As this happened suddenly and unexpectedly, there was no time to collect the people in the villages; moreover, the count who at this time was prefect of the place, viz., the illustrious Bernhar, was absent. The bishop who was there and those who remained in the city and its suburbs, when the first news of their coming arrived, desired to hold the place till further help should reach them ; but when the country people put pressure upon him, and the town was already besieged, he perceived that resistance was impossible, and accordingly made preparations to carry away the sacred relics. As for himself, when his 1clergy had been scattered and had fled in various directions, he with difficulty escaped without even a ,cloak to cover his body. The people left the town and wandered hither and thither; and, whilst most fled away, some were caught, and of these the greater part were killed. The enemy then seized the town and plundered it and its immediate neighborhood. They had come in the evening and they remained that night and the next day and night; and when everything had been burnt and destroyed they took their departure. The church there, which had been built in a wonderful manner under the guidance of the bishop, and the monastery which was also of marvelous construction, were reduced to ashes. The bible which the emperor had given to our father, and which was beautifully transcribed, together with many other books, was lost in the fire. Everything which was used in the services of the Church and all his treasures and possessions were lost by pillage or by fire during the enemy attack. This attack left him practically naked, as nothing had previously been taken away, nor was anything removed at the time except that which each fugitive was able to carry away with him. By none of these things was our holy father distressed, nor did he sin with his lips, but when in a moment of time he lost almost everything that he had been able to gather together, or to collect for purposes of building, he repeated again and again the words of Job [Job 1:21] : "The Lord gave, the Lord has taken away ; the Lord's will has been done. Blessed be the name of the Lord."

CHAPTER XVII.

After these occurrences the bishop continued with his people in their distress and misfortune, whilst the brethren belonging to his Order traversed various districts and wandered hither and thither taking with them the holy relics ; and nowhere did they find rest, owing to the devices of the wicked one. It happened, too, at this time, at the instigation of the devil, that the Swedish people were inflamed with zeal and fury, and began by insidious means to persecute Bishop Gautbert. Thus it came about that some of the people, moved by a common impulse, made a sudden attack upon the house in which he was staying, with the object of destroying it; and in their hatred of the Christian name they killed Nithard, and made him, in our opinion, a true martyr. Gautbert himself and those of his companions who were present they bound, and after plundering everything that they could find in their house, they drove them from their territory with insults and abuse. This was not done by command of the king but was brought about by a plot devised by the people.

CHAPTER XVIII.

The long-suffering mercy of God did not allow this crime to go unavenged, but almost all who were present were soon afterwards punished, though in different ways. Concerning this much might be said, but, lest we should weary our readers, we mention the case of a single individual in order that the destruction which overtook him may show how the rest were also punished and their crimes avenged. In that country there was a certain influential man whose son had joined with the others in this conspiracy, and who had collected in his father's house the booty which he had captured at that Place. Thereafter his possessions began to decrease, and he began to lose his flocks and his household possessions. The son himself was stricken by divine vengeance and died, and after a brief interval his wife, his son and his daughter also died. When the father saw that he had become bereft of all that he had possessed with the exception of one little son, he began, in his misery, to fear the anger of the gods and to imagine that he was suffering all these calamities because he had offended some god. Thereupon, following the local custom, he consulted a soothsayer and asked him to find out by, the casting of lots which god lie had offended and to explain how lie might appease him. After performing all the customary ceremonies, the soothsayer said that all their gods were well disposed towards him, but that the God of the Christians was much incensed against him. " Christ," he said, " has ruined you. It is because there is something hidden in your house which had been consecrated to Him that all the evils that you have suffered have come upon you; nor can you be freed from them as long as this remains in your house." On hearing this he considered anxiously what it could be, and he remembered that his son had brought to his house as part of the aforementioned booty a certain book. On this account he was stricken with horror and fear, and because there was no priest at hand, lie knew not what to do with this book, and, as he dared not keep it any longer in his house, he at length devised a plan and showed the book openly to the people who were in the same hamlet, and told them what he had suffered. When they all said that they knew not how to advise in regard to this matter and were afraid to receive or keep anything of the kind in their houses, he feared greatly to retain it in his own house, and he fastened it up carefully and tied it to a fence with a notice attached stating that whoever wished might take it. For the offence that he had committed he promised also to make voluntary amends to the Lord Jesus Christ. One of the Christians took the book thence and carried it to his own house. This we ascertained from his own statement. Later on he showed such faith and devotion that when with us he learned to say the Psalms without reading them. In like manner were the rest punished, either by death or plague, or by the loss of their property, and it was made manifest to all that they had received due punishment from our Lord Jesus Christ because they had presumed to outrage and plunder God's holy bishop and his companions.

CHAPTER XIX.

For nearly seven years [I.e from 845 to 851] afterwards there was no priest in this place, and for this reason our lord and pastor Ansgar was afflicted with great sorrow, and, as he could not bear that the Christian religion which had begun to be established there should perish, and because he grieved greatly for his dear son Herigar, whom we have already mentioned, he sent a hermit named Ardgar [Adam Brem writes Hardegar] into those parts, and specially directed him to attach himself to Herigar. On his arrival he was courteously received by Herigar and his presence brought great joy to the Christians who were there. These began again to do as they had done before, namely, to search diligently for the things of God and to observe with a willing mind the customs of the Christian religion. None of the unbelievers was able to withstand his preaching, because they remembered with fear the punishment that had come upon those who had expelled God's servants from this Place. On the suggestion of Herigar, and with the command and permission of the king who was then reigning, he began to celebrate the divine mysteries in public. This most faithful man (Herigar) endured many reproaches at the hands of unbelievers during the time when there was no priest present there; but by the help of divine grace and as a result of his prayers the true faith was proclaimed and accompanied by signs from heaven. Some of these, in accordance with our promise [Cf. Chap xi. Finis] have added to our narrative in order that his invincible fidelity may be made manifest.

On one occasion lie himself was sitting in an assembly of people, a stage having been arranged for a council on an open plain. In the course of a general discussion some praised their own gods, by whose favor they had secured great prosperity, whilst others heaped reproaches upon him because he alone, by accepting a worthless creed, had separated himself from them all. He then, being fervent in spirit, is said to have replied, " If there be so great uncertainty in regard to the divine majesty, which nevertheless ought not to be called in doubt by anyone, let us prove by miracles who is the more powerful, the many beings whom ye call your gods or my one Almighty Lord Jesus Christ. See, rain is at hand," a shower was then imminent " call upon the names of your gods and ask that no rain fall upon you, and I will ask my Lord Jesus Christ that not a drop of rain may touch me, and he who on this occasion has regard to those who call upon him let him be God." This was mutually agreed, and as all the rest sat on one side, he and one small boy sat on the other side, and each of them began to invoke his own god, whilst he invoked the Lord Christ. Thereupon a great stream of rain descended, and they were so completely soaked that it seemed as though they and their garments had been thrown into a river. Even the foliage from the branches with which their meeting place had been constructed, fell upon them and thereby proved to them that it was by divine power that they were overcome. On himself and the boy who was with him, not a single drop fell. When this happened, they were confused and astonished. " Ye see," said Herigar, "who is God. Do not, unhappy men, try to draw me away from His worship, but rather be confounded and, renouncing your errors, learn the way of truth." On another occasion it happened that Herigar was suffering great pain in his leg, so that it was impossible for him to move out of his place except when he was carried. When lie had endured this distress for some time, many persons came to visit him, some of whom urged him to sacrifice to the gods in order to regain his health, whilst others assailed him with jeers, saying that his illness was due to the fact that he had no god. When this had occurred on several occasions and he had strenuously resisted their evil suggestions, and when at length lie could no longer bear their reproaches, he replied that he would not seek aid from vain images but from his Lord Jesus Christ who, if he wished, could cure him in a moment of his sickness. He then summoned his servants and told them to carry him to his church. When he had been placed there he poured out his supplications to the Lord in the presence of all the bystanders and said : "My Lord Jesus Christ grant to me thy servant now my former health in order that these unhappy men may know that Thou art the only God and that there is none beside Thee, and in order that my enemies may behold the great things that Thou doest, and may turn in confusion from their errors and be converted to the knowledge of Thy name. Accomplish, I beseech Thee, that which I ask for the sake of Thy holy name, which is blessed for evermore, that they who believe in Thee may not be confounded, O Lord." Having said this, he was forthwith healed by the grace of God, and was made completely well. He, accordingly, left the church unaided and rendered thanks to God for his health, and strengthened in the faith of Christ, he more and more confounded those who disbelieved.

About the same time, it happened that a certain Swedish king named Anoundus had been driven from his kingdom and was an exile amongst the Danes. Desiring to regain what had once been his kingdom, he sought their aid and promised that if they would follow him they would be able to secure much treasure. He offered them Birka, the town already mentioned, because it contained many rich merchants, and a large amount of goods and money. He promised to lead them to this place where, without much loss to their army, they might gain what they wanted. Enticed by the promised gifts and eager to acquire treasure, they filled twenty-one ships with men ready for battle and placed them at his disposal; moreover, he had eleven of his own ships. These left Denmark and came unexpectedly upon the above-mentioned town. It so happened that the king [I.e. Biorn] of the town was absent, and the chiefs and people were unable to meet together. Only Herigar, the prefect of this place, was present with the merchants and people who remained there. Being in great difficulty they fled to a neighboring town [I.e. Sigtuna] and began to promise and offer to their gods, who were demons, many vows and sacrifices in order that by their help they might be preserved in so great a peril. But inasmuch as the town was not strong and there were few to offer resistance, they sent messengers to the Danes and asked for friendship and alliance. The king [I.e. Anoundus] beforementioned commanded them to pay a hundred pounds of silver in order to redeem Birka and obtain peace. They forthwith sent the amount asked and it was received by the king. The Danes resented this agreement, because it was not in accord with their arrangement, and they wanted to make a sudden attack upon them and to pillage and burn the place because they said that each individual merchant in the place had more than had been offered to them and they could not endure that such a trick should be played upon them. As they were discussing this and were preparing to destroy the town to which the others had fled, their design became known to those in the town. They gathered together then, a second time and, as they possessed no power of resistance and had no hope of securing refuge, they exhorted one another to make vows and to offer greater sacrifices to their own gods. Herigar, the faithful servant of the Lord, was angry with them and said, " Your vows and sacrifices to idols are accursed by God. How long will ye serve devils and injure and impoverish yourselves by your useless vows. You have made many offerings and more vows and have given a hundred pounds of silver. What benefit has it been to you? See, your enemies are coming to destroy all that you have. They will lead away your wives and sons as captives, they will burn our city and town [I.e. Sigtuna and Birka] and will destroy you with the sword. Of what advantage are your idols to you "? As he said this they were all terrified and, as they knew not what to do, they replied all together It is for you to devise plans for our safety, and whatever you suggest we will not fail to perform." He replied: "If you desire to make vows, vow and perform your vows to the Lord God omnipotent, who reigns in heaven, and whom I serve with a pure conscience and a trite faith. He is Lord of all, and all things are subject to His will, nor can anyone resist His decree. If then ye will seek His help with your whole heart ye shall perceive that His omnipotent power will not fail you." They accepted his advice and in accordance with custom, they all went out of their own accord to a plain where they promised the Lord Christ to fast and to give alms in order to secure their deliverance. Meanwhile the king proposed to the Danes that they should enquire by casting lots whether it was the will of the gods that this place should be ravaged by them. " There are there," he said, " many great and powerful gods, and in former time a church was built there, and there are many Christians there who worship Christ, who is the strongest of the gods and can aid those who hope in Him, in any way that He chooses.

THE LIFE OF ST. ANSGAR

We must seek to ascertain therefore whether it is by the will of the gods that we are urged to make this attempt." As his words were in accord with their custom they could not refuse to adopt the suggestion. Accordingly, they sought to discover the will of the gods by casting lots and they ascertained that it would be impossible to accomplish their purpose without endangering their own welfare and that God would not permit this place to be ravaged by them. They asked further where they should go in order to obtain money for themselves so that they might not have to return home without having gained that for which they had hoped. They ascertained by the casting of the lot that they ought to go to a certain town which was situated at a distance on the borders of the lands belonging to the Slavonians. The Danes then, believing that this order had come to them from heaven, retired from this place and hastened to go by a direct route to that town. Having made a sudden attack upon its people, who were living in quiet and peace, they seized it by force of arms and, having captured much spoil and treasure, they returned home. Moreover, the king who had come with the object of plundering the Swedes, made peace with them and restored the money that he had recently received from them. He remained also for some time with them as he wished to become reconciled to their nation. Thus did the good Lord, on account of the faith of his servant Herigar, free the people of this place from the attack of their enemies and restore to them their possessions. After these occurrences Herigar brought forward a proposal in a public assembly and advised that they should try more earnestly to ascertain who was God. " Alas, wretched people," he said, " ye now understand that it is useless to seek for help from demons who cannot succour those who are in trouble. Accept the faith of my Lord Jesus Christ, whom ye have proved to be the true God and who in His compassion has brought solace to you who have no refuge from sorrow. Seek not any more after superstitious worship, or to appease your idols by useless sacrifice. Worship the true God who rules all things in heaven and earth, submit yourselves to Him, and adore His almighty power. His own faith having been strengthened by the abounding goodness of the Lord, he was the more ready to come forward both publicly and otherwise, and at one time by reproach, at another time by persuasion, he declared unto them the power of the Lord and the benefits resulting from faith in Him. And thus, he continued the good fight even to the end of his life.

When at length his good deeds were complete and his weakness had increased, having been commended to the mercy of God in the presence of the priest Ardgar, and having received the Holy Communion, he departed this life happily in Christ. Much more might be said concerning the constancy of his faith, but this must suffice, inasmuch as we desire our narrative to be brief.

CHAPTER XX.

At that time there was amongst the Swedes a very pious matron, whom the frowardness of wicked men had been unable to turn aside from the true faith. It was frequently suggested to her, when she was placed in any difficult position, that she should, in accordance with their custom, offer sacrifices to idols, but she remained unmoved and did not abandon the performance of her religious duties, She declared that it was useless to seek for help from dumb and deaf images and that she thought it detestable to do again the things that she had renounced in her baptism and to fail to perform the promise that she had made to Christ. If it be an evil thing to lie to men how much worse is it to lie to God? And if it be a good thing that faith should be preserved amongst men how much greater is the obligation that rests upon one who receives the faith of the Lord to continue firm and not to mingle falsehood with truth? "The Lord," she said, " even my Jesus Christ, is omnipotent, and if I continue to believe in Him, He can give me health and everything that I need according to His good pleasure." This devout woman, whose name was Frideburg, who was deserving of praise for the goodness of her life and the constancy of her faith, continued even to old age. When she believed that the day of her death was approaching, and no priest had come there since the death of Gautbert, desiring the due performance of the ceremony [Codex Ambianensis adds "sacrificii"] which she had heard was the "viaticum" of Christians, she caused some wine that she had bought to be reserved in a certain vessel. She further requested her daughter, who was also a devout woman, that when her last moments came, as she had not the sacrifice she should drop some of the wine into her mouth and thus commend her departure to the mercy of the Lord. She kept this wine with her for nearly three years by which time the priest Ardgar had arrived there. After his appointment she performed her religious duties as long as she retained her strength, and she sought at his hands the customary rites and helpful admonition. Meanwhile weakness overtook her and she became sick. Being anxious, in view of her death, she caused the priest to be summoned, and having received from his hand the viaticum she departed with joy to the Lord She had ever been intent on almsgiving and, as she was rich in this world's goods, she had enjoined her daughter Catla [Codex Amb. reads Cathle.] that, after her departure from this life, she should distribute all that she possessed amongst the poor. " And because," she said, "there are here but few poor, at the first opportunity that occurs after my death, sell all that has not been given away and go with the money to Dorstadt. There are there many churches, priests, and clergy, and a multitude of poor people. On your arrival seek out faithful persons who may teach you how to distribute this and give away everything as alms for the benefit of my soul." After the death of her mother the daughter diligently accomplished everything that she had ordered.

She took her journey to Dorstadt, and on her arrival she sought out some devout women who accompanied her to the holy places in the town and told her what to give to each person. On a certain day as they were visiting the holy places for the purpose of distributing charity, when half had already been distributed, she said to her companion, " We are already weary, we had better buy some wine wherewith to refresh ourselves so that we may accomplish the work that we have begun. She provided, therefore, four denarii for this purpose and having recovered their strength they finished their task. When it was completed and she was returning to her lodging, she placed the empty bag which had contained the money, in a certain spot, but, as a result of divine intervention, when she came again to the spot she found that the bag was as full as it had been before. Amazed at so great a miracle, she summoned the devout women who had gone with her and explained to them what had happened to her. In their presence she reckoned up the money that was in the bag and found that it was exactly the sum that she had brought thither with the exception of the four denarii. At their suggestion she went to the priests who were of repute in that place and told them what had happened. They rendered thanks to God for His great goodness and said that the Lord had thus repaid her toil and her good intention. " Forasmuch," they said, " as you have obeyed your mother and have kept your pledge to her unimpaired, and, by undertaking this toilsome journey, have accomplished her generous purpose, the Lord of all good, who repays and rewards, hath given you this in order to supply your own needs. He is almighty and self-sufficient and is in need of nothing. He will repay in His heavenly kingdom everything that is distributed by His faithful followers to supply the needs of the poor and of His servants. The Lord hath deigned to assure you by a miracle that this is so, lest you should doubt or repent having distributed your treasure. By this same sign be assured that thy mother is safe with the Lord, and, admonished by this miracle, fear not to give up your property for the sake of Christ, knowing that the Lord will repay you in heaven. This is God's gift to you, and it is for you to distribute in accordance with your own will. That which you have taken and used for your own purposes He would not restore, for in His kindness He gave back only that which out of love for Him had been distributed amongst the poor."

The priest Ardgar, after the death of Herigar, then moved by the desire to lead a solitary life as he had formerly done, departed from those parts and sought again his own place. Thus were the Christians who lived here deprived once again of the presence of a priest. In this way it became clearly manifest that the hermit Ardgar had been providentially sent to these parts in order that he might strengthen the faith of Herigar and of the matron above mentioned and might commend their departure to the mercy of God and that, in accordance with their constant desire, they might receive the sacrament of the Holy Communion to serve as their final viaticum.

CHAPTER XXI.

While the events above related were occurring, it came to pass by divine ordering that the emperor Ludovic, of happy memory, departed this life. [He died on June 20th, 840] When, after his death, a great disturbance arose in connection with the division of the kingdom the status of our pastor as an (imperial) delegate was weakened. For when the above mentioned monastery of Turholt had come into the possession of King Charles, he set it free from the servitude which his father had ordained and gave it to Raginar, who is well known to you. On this account his brothers, the most noble kings, and many others also besought him frequently, but he refused to heed their requests, and our father began to be worried by many needs and distresses. Thus, it came about that your brethren who were with him here [That is at Hamburg] at that time returned to your society and many others also left him on the ground of poverty. He, however, continued to live as he best could with the few who remained with him; and, though he was very poor, he would not abandon the task that had been assigned to him.

CHAPTER XXII.

When the Lord beheld his humility and his patient courage inasmuch as the heart of the king is in the hand of the Lord He stirred up the mind of our most gracious lord and ruler King Ludovic, who took charge of the kingdom after his father's death, and incited him to discover how he might secure for him a comfortable subsistence, so that lie might accomplish the trust committed to him. And because he possessed no monastery in this province suitable for this purpose, he arranged to give him the bishopric of Bremen, which was near at hand and was at that time without a pastor. Accordingly, at a public meeting of bishops and of his other faithful servants he discussed with them whether canonical law would permit of his doing this. For our lord and pastor, fearful lest this should prove dangerous to himself, and in order to guard against being blamed by any for covetousness, did not readily assent to this arrangement. By command of the king this matter was threshed out in the council of bishops. They showed by many precedents that it could easily be done, inasmuch as the diocese to which lie had been ordained was very small it had only four churches in which baptisms were held. Moreover, this diocese had been many times devastated by the incursions of barbarians, and on this account, they urged that it should be joined to the diocese of Bremen in order to afford him relief. But in order that the Bishop of Verden might not suffer injury if lie (Ansgar) were to retain, in addition to the whole of the Bremen diocese, that part of his own diocese which lay beyond the river Elbe, and which had been taken away, they decided that, as there had been the two dioceses of Bremen and Verden in the time of the Emperor Ludovic these should be restored and that Ansgar should keep Bremen, out of which the greater part of his own diocese had been taken, the diocese of Bremen being at that time bereft of a pastor. [Cf. Adam Brm. I., Chap xxiv]

When this decision had been confirmed by the bishops lie undertook, at the command of the king, to govern the diocese of Bremen; whilst Waldgar the Bishop of Verden, took over that part of his own diocese which lay beyond the river Elbe. After this had been settled the matter was again carefully discussed in a council of bishops who thought that it was not right that the episcopal see to which be had been ordained should be held by another bishop for Hammaburg had at that time fallen to the share of Waldgar. They said, moreover, that it was within the king's rights to extend a small diocese and one which had been devastated, but that a place to which archiepiscopal rank had been attached by apostolic authority ought, on no account, to be transferred. With the approval of the most pious King Ludovic the bishops who were there present, unanimously decided that our father Ansgar should receive the see to which lie had been consecrated, and that if be retained any territory beyond the river Elbe that belonged to the diocese of Verden, he should make restitution to the bishop of that diocese out of the diocese of Bremen. This was carried into effect by the command of the king and by the decree of the episcopal synod, with the approval and consent of Waldgar, the Bishop of Verden.

CHAPTER XXIII.

When these things were being done the town of Cologne to which the diocese of Bremen was subject, was at that time bereft of a bishop. And as this had been the case for some time, this matter had to be decided without the presence of a bishop of this place. When later on the Venerable Gunthar had been consecrated as bishop of this place [Gunther was consecrated on May 20th, 850], our lord and father desired to put the matter before him so that it might be confirmed by his authority. Gunthar, however, was opposed to this scheme. For this reason, at a council held by the two kings Ludovic and Lothair, at Worms, at which there were present many bishops belonging to both kingdoms, including our venerable father, the same matter was brought forward. When this decision had been universally approved they all asked Bishop Gunthar to confirm and sanction it. He was at first strenuously opposed to them, and declared in many words that it was not right that a suffragan see should be transformed into an archbishopric, or that the dignity of his own see should be in any respect diminished. At length, however, when the kings and all the bishops present besought this of him, saying that it was lawful because it was necessary, lie replied that he would ratify the proposal

THE LIFE OF ST. ANSGAR

provided that it were supported by apostolic authority. When this reply had been received and all his suffragans had agreed, King Ludovic, who desired to extend the charitable purpose of his father and that the arrangement which lie had made should be completely established, sent the most reverend Bishop Salomon, the Bishop of Constanz [Salamon was bishop of Constanz from 839 to 871] to the apostolic see in order to promote this object. With him our lord and father Ansgar, as he could not go himself, sent his son, [Cf. Chap xix, not.] our brother, the priest Nordfrid. These were most kindly received by the most holy Pope Nicholas [Nicholas I, who was pope from 858 to 867] and to him they explained fully and clearly the mission with which they had been entrusted. He considered with wisdom and care the things which they told him, and, as he perceived by the help of God that this arrangement would conduce to the winning of the souls of these races, he confirmed by his own authority the wish expressed by our king. In order that we may the more clearly explain the matter, which was carefully elucidated by him, we have determined to give his own words. After he had fully and at the same time briefly recapitulated the reason for the sending of the messengers by the king, and other matters which we have included in our previous account, he went on to say : " The written statement relating to the authority of the messengers, and to the reception of the pallium, which was sent to us from our son Ludovic by the hand of the most holy Bishop Salomon, was authenticated in accordance with the custom of the holy Roman Church.

From the contents of his written statement, we find that matters are even as the pious king made known to us by his trusty messenger Bishop Salomon. We therefore, following in the steps of our predecessor, the great Bishop Gregory, and recognising that the arrangements made by his foresight were deserving of divine approval, have decided to sanction the wish expressed by the great chiefs, viz., the Emperor Ludovic, of sacred memory, and his most excellent son, who bore the same name, by a writing bearing apostolic authority and by the presentation of the pallium in accordance with the custom of our predecessors. In order that Ansgar may he authoritatively established as the first archbishop of the Northalbingians, and that his successors, who strive for the salvation of the nations, may be strong to resist the attack of the evil one, we appoint our son Ansgar as our legate amongst all the surrounding races of Swedes, Danes and Slavs, and amongst all others living in those parts, whichever the grace of God may open a way, and we grant him authority to preach the gospel openly.

We decree also that Hamburg, the see of the North Albingians, which has been dedicated to our holy Saviour and to Mary His undefiled Mother, should henceforth be an archiepiscopal see. We call God to witness that we decree this in order that after the death of the great preacher, Archbishop Ansgar, there may ever hereafter be chosen persons worthy of this great office. But inasmuch as King Charles, the brother of Ludovic, after the death of his father the emperor, Ludovic, of pious memory, took away from Hamburg the monastery called Turholt, which his father had given to the bishop and his clergy in order to supply them with food and other necessaries, all those who ministered at the altar began to leave the place, because, after the division of the kingdom between the two brothers, it appeared to lie within his kingdom, being situated in Western France.

When the necessary funds were no longer available they left these races, and the mission to them which had been carried on in this way, ceased: even the metropolis, Hamburg, was well-nigh deserted. While these events were taking place the Bishop of Bremen, the diocese of which is said to be contiguous to this see, died. When the king perceived that this diocese was without a bishop and that the newly instituted diocese had been weakened, and that in addition the churches in both dioceses had been enfeebled by the savagery displayed by the barbarians, he began to ask whether the diocese of Bremen might be united and made subject to the new archiepiscopal see and whether his project might be authorized by our decree. Accordingly, this matter was referred to us by his messenger Salomon, the venerable Bishop of Constanz, in order that we might approve it and we were asked to confirm the same by our authority. We, therefore, after carefully weighing and considering the proposal, think that it will be advantageous in view of the pressing need and in order to win souls amongst the heathen. For we doubt not that all things that are proved to be profitable to the Church and which are not opposed to divine ordinances are lawful and ought to be done, especially in a district in which the faith has so recently been introduced and in which many different issues are wont to arise. Wherefore, by the authority of Almighty God and the blessed apostles Peter and Paul, and by this our decree we decide, in accordance with the wish of King Ludovic, that these dioceses of Hamburg and Bremen shall henceforth be called not two dioceses but one diocese, and that they shall be subject to the see which was raised to archiepiscopal rank by the decree of our predecessor, provided that the diocese of Ferden receive back from the Church of Bremen that territory which before had been taken away. No archbishop of Cologne shall henceforth lay claim to any authority in this diocese. Moreover we exhort him and all who accept the true faith to assist and support those who carry out this commission, so that for their good deeds they may deserve to receive full reward from Him who said: ' Go and teach all the nations," [Matt xxviii.19] and 'whosoever receiveth you receiveth me.' [Matt. X.40] We confirm by our authority therefore, all the wishes expressed by our beloved son King Ludovic, relating to this important matter. And inasmuch as what has happened in the past renders us cautious for the future, we smite with the sword of our anathema everyone who opposes, or contradicts, or tries to interfere with this our desire, and we condemn him to share with the devil everlasting vengeance. We do this in accordance with the custom of our predecessors and in our pious zeal for God, in order that we may render the exalted apostolic see more secure against the attack of all enemies."

By the decrees and dispositions of the holy Pope Nicholas, the Church of Bremen was joined and united to the see of Hamburg, which had formerly been made a metropolitical see and now became an archbishopric.

CHAPTER XXIV.

But inasmuch as we have spoken in advance concerning the arrangements that were made relating to this diocese for a long time elapsed after Ansgar had undertaken the government of this see before it was settled by apostolic authority let us now go back to the events of an earlier period. For after he took over the diocese of Bremen and became possessed of some resources he began once more to desire vehemently that, if it were possible, he might labour on Christ's behalf amongst the Danes. For this reason he paid frequent visits to Horic, who was at that time sole monarch of the Danes, and endeavored to conciliate him by gifts and by any possible kinds of service in the hope that he might gain permission to preach in his kingdom. On several occasions he was sent to him as an ambassador of the king and sought strenuously and faithfully to bring about a peace that should be advantageous to either kingdom. His fidelity and goodness having been thus recognized, King Horic began to regard him with great affection and to make use of his advice and to treat him in every respect as a friend; so that he was allowed to share his secrets when with his fellow counsellors he was dealing with matters relating to the kingdom. As concerning the matters which had to be arranged in order to establish an alliance between the people of this land, that is the Saxons, and his own kingdom, the king only desired that it should be guaranteed by his pledge, as he said that he had complete confidence; regard to everything that lie approved and promised. When Ansgar had thus gained his friendship, he began to urge him to become a Christian. The king listened to all that he told him out of the Holy Scriptures and declared that it was both good and helpful and that he took great delight therein, and that lie desired to earn the favor of Christ. After he had expressed these desires our good father suggested to him that he grant to the Lord Christ that which would he most pleasing to Him, namely, permission to build a church in his kingdom, where a priest might always be present who might commit to those who were willing to receive them the seeds of the Divine Word and the grace of baptism. The king most kindly granted this permission and allowed him to build a church in a part belonging to his kingdom, called Sliaswic, which was specially suitable for this purpose and was near to the district where merchants from all parts congregated ; he gave also a place in which a priest might five, and likewise granted permission to anyone in his kingdom who desired to become a Christian. When our lord bishop obtained this permission, he at once did that which he had long desired. And when a priest had been established there, the grace of God began to bear much fruit in that place, for there were many who had already become Christians and had been baptized in Dorstadt or Hamburg, amongst whom were the principal people of the place, who rejoiced at the opportunity afforded them to observe their religion. Many others also, both men and women, followed their example, and having abandoned the superstitious worship of idols. believed in the Lord and were baptized. There was, moreover, great joy in that place, as the men of this place could now do what was before forbidden, and traders both from here [That is Hamburg] and from Dorstadt freely sought to visit this place, [Schleswig] and opportunity was afforded for doing much good there. And whilst many who were baptized there have survived, an innumerable host of those who were clothed in white have ascended to the heavenly kingdom. For they were willingly signed with the cross in order to become catechumens, and that they might enter the church and be present at the sacred offices ; but they deferred the reception of baptism, as they judged that it was to their advantage to be baptized at the end of their life, so that, having been cleansed by water unto salvation, they might without any delay enter the gates of eternal life as those who were pure and spotless. Many also amongst them, who were overcome with sickness, when they saw that their sacrifices offered to idols in order to secure their recovery were of no avail, and when their neighbors despaired of their getting well, took refuge in the Lord's mercy and vowed that they would become Christians. When a priest had been summoned and they had received the grace of baptism, by divine help they forthwith recovered their health. In such wise did the divine compassion spread in that place and a multitude of people were converted unto the Lord. [The period covered would be from 848 to 852]

CHAPTER XXV.

Meanwhile our lord and master Ansgar being greatly distressed on behalf of the Swedish race because it was at that time without a priest, begged King Horic, who was his intimate friend, that he might with his help make an effort to reach this kingdom. The king received this request with the utmost goodwill and promised that he would do everything to help. Accordingly, the bishop began to negotiate with Bishop Gautbert, [at this time bishop of Osnabrück; he died in 845] saying that a further attempt must be made to discover whether this race, having been divinely admonished, would permit priests to dwell amongst them, so that the Christian faith, which had been established in those parts, might not perish in consequence of their neglect. Bishop Gautbert, who is also called Simon, replied that, as he had been expelled from that country, he would not venture to go thither again, and that the attempt could not be advantageous, but would on the contrary be dangerous, should those who remembered what happened before raise a disturbance about him. He said that it seemed to him to be more fitting that lie should go who was the first to undertake this mission and who had been kindly treated there, and that he would send with him his nephew [Erimebert, see chap xxviii] who might remain there, should he find opportunity for preaching, and might perform the duties of a priest amongst the people. When they had so decided, they came to King Ludovic and told begged that he him the reason for their action and would permit them to do this. He asked whether they themselves had come to an agreement, whereupon the venerable Bishop Gautbert replied: " In the service of God we are ' and have always been, united, and it is our unanimous desire that this should be done." Accordingly, the king, who was ever ready to further God's work, enjoined this mission upon our holy father, in accordance with the terms they had agreed among themselves, and on his part entrusted to the bishop injunctions addressed to the king of Sweden, as his father had done before. Our good father then began to prepare for this journey and became the more eager to accomplish it with the utmost speed. Moreover, he believed that he was commanded by heaven to undertake it, as he was influenced by a vision which he had before seen. For in the vision lie thought that he was anxious in view of this very journey and it seemed to him that lie came to a place where there were large buildings and dwellings of different kinds. A certain man met him there and said, " Do not be overmuch distressed, for the journey concerning which you are anxious, for there is a certain prophet in this place who will inform you concerning all these matters. And lest in regard to this matter any hesitation should take possession of your mind, I will tell you who this prophet is: Adalhard, the once famous abbot, is the prophet whom the Lord hath sent to you to tell you the things that are to come to pass." Being greatly encouraged by what he heard in his vision, Ansgar replied: " Where shall I find him, O Lord? " " You will find him," was the reply, " by your own effort, and no one may bring him to you." Then it seemed to him that he passed round the dwellings seeking for him and at the same time he said to himself, " If without my asking him he shall tell me what is in my mind, then I shall be satisfied that he is a true prophet." He went on then to a bright and beautiful dwelling and saw him sitting on his chair and recognized him forthwith. He (the prophet) looked upon him and said immediately: " Hear, 0 islands, and give ear ye peoples from afar. The Lord bath called thee from the womb and from thy mother's belly; he bath remembered thy name and he hath made thy mouth as a sharp sword and bath covered thee with the shadow of his hand and hath made thee like a choice arrow. He hath hidden thee in his quiver, and hath said unto thee, ' Thou art my servant, for in thee I will be glorified.' " [Isaiah xlix, 1-3] Having said this he stretched out his arm and lifted his right hand to him. When Ansgar saw this he advanced to his knees hoping that he would be willing to bless him. But he added these words, " Now saith the Lord that formed thee from the womb to be his servant, I have given thee to be a light to the Gentiles that thou mayest be unto them salvation even to the end of the earth. Kings shall see and princes shall rise up together and they shall worship the Lord thy God, even the Holy One of Israel, for lie shall glorify thee." [Isaiah xlix., 5-7]

God's servant, having beheld this vision long before he set out on his journey, was assured that he was summoned by a divine command to go to those parts, and specially by the word that had been spoken " Hear, O islands," because almost all that country consisted of islands ; and by that which had been added, " Thou shalt be unto them for salvation, even unto the end of the earth," because in the north the end of the world lay in Swedish territory. Finally the word quoted from the end of Jeremiah's [A mistake for Isaiah] prophecy: "For He shall glorify thee," encouraged his eager desire, as he thought that this referred to the crown of martyrdom that had once been promised to him.

CHAPTER XXVI.

As he was then about to set out on this journey [I.e. probably in 852. See Dreves, p. 99.n] he took with him the message and the token [See chap xii] given him by King Horic, who directed him to give the message to the Swedish king named Olef and to say that the messenger whom King Ludovic had sent to his kingdom was well known to him and that he had never before in his life seen so good a man, nor had ever found any other human being so trustworthy. In recognition of his goodness he had allowed him to do whatever he wished in his kingdom in the interests of the Christian religion, and he (King Ludovic) begged that he would permit him to establish the Christian religion in his own kingdom, as he (Ansgar) desired, for he would do nothing that would not be good and right. Ansgar accomplished the journey on which he had set out, and after spending nearly twenty days in a ship, he arrived at Birka, where he found that the king and many of the people were perplexed by grievous errors. It happened, at the instigation of the devil, who knew beforehand of the coming of this good man, that someone had come thither and said that he had been present at a meeting of the gods, who were believed to be the owners of this land, and had been sent by them to make this announcement to the king and the people : " You, I say, have long enjoyed our goodwill, and under our protection the land in which you dwell has long been fertile and has had peace and prosperity. You have also duly sacrificed and performed the vows made to us, and your worship has been well pleasing to us. But now you are keeping back the usual sacrifices and are slothful in paying your freewill offerings; you are, moreover, displeasing us greatly by introducing a foreign god in order to supplant us. If you desire to enjoy our goodwill, offer the sacrifices that have been omitted and pay greater vows. And do not receive the worship of any other god, who teaches that which is opposed to our teaching, nor pay any attention to his service. Furthermore, if you desire to have more gods and we do not suffice, we will agree to summon your former King Eric [I.e. Eric III, the predecessor of Biörn] to join us so that he may be one of the gods." This devilish announcement, which was publicly made on the arrival of the bishop, disturbed the minds of all, and their hearts were deceived and disquieted. For they had resolved to have a temple in honor of the late king, and bad begun to render votive offerings and sacrifices to him as to a god. When then, the bishop came thither, he asked his friends whom he had formerly known there how he might speak to the king on this matter. They all, with one accord, deprecated his doing so, and said that for the time being this mission could effect nothing, and that if he had anything of value with him be should give it to the king so that he might escape with his life. He replied, " For the saving of my life would I give nothing, for, if my Lord shall so ordain, I am ready to submit to torments and to suffer death for His name." Being in great uncertainty in regard to this matter, he acted on the advice that lie received, and invited the king to partake of his hospitality. Then, as a fellowguest, he offered what gifts he could and gave him the things with which he had been entrusted, for the cause of his coming had already been explained to the king by Horic's messenger, and by the bishop's friends who resided there. The king was delighted with his kindness and liberality and said that he gladly agreed to what he had proposed. " In former time," he said, " there have been clergy who have been driven out by a rising of the people and not by the command of the king. On this account I have not the power, nor do I dare, to approve the objects of your mission until I can consult our gods by the casting of lots and until I can enquire the will of the people in regard to this matter. Let your messenger attend with me the next assembly [See chap xix, note] and I will speak to the people on your behalf. And if they approve your desire and the gods consent, that which you have asked shall be successfully carried out, but if it should turn out otherwise, I will let you know. It is our custom that the control of public business of every kind should rest with the whole people and not with the king." When our good pastor received the king's reply he turned to the Lord for refuge, and gave up his time to fasting and prayer, and with heartfelt contrition he humbled himself before God.

CHAPTER XXVII.

While he was in this difficult position and the time for the assembly drew near, he was one day engaged in the service of the Mass, and while the priest was standing by the altar and was blessing the sacred mysteries, a divine inspiration came upon him as he prostrated himself on the ground.

THE LIFE OF ST. ANSGAR

Strengthened then, by the gift of the Holy Spirit, and endued with the most complete confidence, he recognized that all would turn out as he desired. Accordingly, when the Mass was finished, he declared to this same priest, who was his most intimate associate, that he ought to have no fear, for God Himself would be his helper. When the priest asked how he knew this he replied that his knowledge was divinely inspired. The brother was able to recognize this divine illumination, as he knew that he had been divinely inspired in many previous instances, and the result speedily justified his confidence. As soon as his chiefs were assembled the king began to discuss with them the mission on which our father had come. They determined that enquiry should be made by the casting of lots in order to discover what was the will of the gods. They went out, therefore, to the plain, in accordance with their custom, and the lot [Cf. Chap xix note] decided that it was the will of God that the Christian religion should be established there. When this happened, one of the chief men, who was a friend of the bishop, told him forthwith and bade him be comforted, and said, "Be strong and act with vigor, for God has not denied your wish nor rejected your mission." He then became of good courage and rejoicing in spirit exulted in the Lord. When the day for the assembly which was held in the town of Birka drew near, in accordance with their national custom the king caused a proclamation to be made to the people by the voice of a herald, in order that they might be informed concerning the object of their mission. On hearing this, those who had before been led astray into error, held discordant and confused opinions. In the midst of the noise and confusion one of the older men amongst them said: "Listen to me, O king and people. In regard to the worship of this God it is well known to many of us that He can afford much help to those who place their hope in Him. For many of us have proved this to be the case on several occasions when in peril by sea and in other crises. Why, then, do we reject that which we know to be both needful and serviceable? Some of us who on various occasions have been to Dorstadt have of our own accord adopted this form of religion, believing it to be beneficial. Our way thither is now beset by those who lie in wait for us and is rendered dangerous by the attacks of pirates. Why then do we not take that which is brought to us and which, when it was at a distance, we sought eagerly to obtain? We, who have frequently proved that the help afforded by this God can be useful to us, why should we not gladly agree to continue as his servants? Consider carefully, O people, and do not cast away that which will be to your advantage. For, inasmuch as we cannot be sure that our gods will be favorably disposed, it is good for us to have the help of this God who is always, and under all circumstances able and willing to succor those who cry to Him." When he had finished speaking all the people unanimously decided that the priests should remain with them, and that everything that pertained to the performance of the Christian mysteries should be done without let or hindrance. The king then rose up from amongst the assembly and forthwith directed one of his own messengers to accompany the bishop's messenger, and to tell him that the people were unanimously inclined to accept his proposal and at the same time to tell him that, whilst their action was entirely agreeable to him, he could not give his full consent until, in another assembly, which was to be held in another part of his kingdom, he could announce this resolution to the people who lived in that district. Once again, then, our good father sought, as was his custom, for divine assistance, and eagerly besought God's mercy. When the time for the assembly came and the king had caused to be proclaimed by the voice of a herald the object for which the bishop had come, and all that had been said and done at the previous assembly, by divine providence the hearts of all became as one, so that they adopted the resolution passed by the former assembly and declared that they too would give their entire and complete assent.

CHAPTER XXVIII.

When this had been done the king summoned the bishop and told him what had occurred. The king, accordingly, with the goodwill and approval of all, determined that churches might be built among the people, and that priests might come to them and that whoever so desired might become a Christian without let or hindrance. Our lord and pastor then commended to the care of the King Erimbert the nephew of the venerable Bishop Gautbert, in order that, with his help and protection, he might there perform the sacred mysteries, and to him the king granted permission to build a hall to serve as a place of prayer in the town already mentioned ; the bishop also bought another courtyard, together with a house in which the priest might live. The king displayed further his affectionate regard for the lord bishop and promised that in every district he would show the utmost kindness to his companions who were concerned with the observance of the Christian religion. When then, by the Lord's grace everything had been duly accomplished the bishop returned to his own house.

CHAPTER XXIX.

While preparations were being made for his journey [I.e. to Sweden] our good father foresaw in advance, by divine revelation, the mental anguish which he afterwards endured during his journey ; for one night he saw, as in a vision, that it was the time of our Lord's passion and that he was himself present when the Lord Jesus Christ was led from Pilate to Herod, and again from Herod to Pilate, arid when He endured the spitting and insults at the hands of the Jews and the soldiers, and it seemed to him that he was himself scourged all over because he would not stiffer Him to be so punished, but came forward and gave his back to the scourgers and received in his own body the blows that were inflicted on Him, His head only being excepted because, being taller of stature, He seemed to reach beyond him and he could not therefore protect His head. Christ's invincible soldier did not understand what this meant till, on his return from this journey, he considered how much insult and derision he had borne arid in what great straits he had been placed and what blasphemies against God he had there endured. For, in so far as he was himself concerned, he undoubtedly suffered there on Christ's behalf and Christ in His servant bore again the reproaches that were directed against Himself. Furthermore, he thought that the fact that he was not able to protect His head signified that the head of Christ is God and the sufferings which the saints endure in this world on Christ's behalf, pertain in part to the majesty of God who, in virtue of His sympathy, endures them for a time, but will someday severely judge, even as it is written Vengeance is mine, I will repay, saith the Lord." [Rom xii., 19: Heb. X.so: Deut xxxii., 35f]

CHAPTER XXX.

Nor should we omit to mention how, after the completion of this journey, the power of the Lord was manifested to the Swedes. For a certain people named Cori had in former time been in subjection to the Swedes but had a long while since rebelled and refused to be in subjection. The Danes, being aware of this, at the time when the bishop had come into Swedish territory, collected a large number of ships, and proceeded to this country, eager to seize their goods and to subject them to themselves. Their kingdom contained five towns, When the inhabitants knew of their coming, they gathered together arid began to resist manfully and to defend their property. I laving obtained the victory they massacred half the Danes arid plundered their ships, obtaining from them gold and silver and much spoil. On hearing this, King Olaf and the Swedes, who wished to win for themselves the reputation that they could do what the Danes had not done, and because this people had formerly been subject to them, collected an immense army arid proceeded to these parts. In the first instance they came to a town in their kingdom called Seeburg. This town, which contained seven thousand fighting men, they ravaged and despoiled and burnt. They left it with strengthened hopes and, having sent away their ships, set out on a five days journey arid hastened with savage intent to another of their towns called Aputra in which there were fifteen thousand fighting men. When they reached it, these were shut up in the town, and whilst one party vigorously attacked the town from outside, the other party defended it from within. In this way eight days went by with the result that, though they fought and waged war from morning till night, and many fell on both sides, neither side obtained the victory. On the ninth day the Swedes, being exhausted by the daily slaughter, began to be distressed, and in their terror considered only how they might get away. "Here," they said, we effect nothing, and we are far from our ships." For, as we have said, it was five days' journey to the port which contained their ships. As they were greatly disturbed and knew not what they should do, they resolved to enquire by casting lots whether their gods were willing to aid them either to obtain a victory or to get away from the place where they were. Having cast lots they failed to discover any god who was willing to aid them. And when this was announced to the people there arose much outcry and lamentation in their camp, and all their courage left them. "What," said they, " shall we, unhappy people, do? The gods have departed from us and none of them will aid us. Whither shall we flee? Our ships are far away, and if we flee (those in the city) will follow after us and will utterly destroy us. What hope have we? " When they were in this great difficulty some merchants, who remembered the teaching and instruction given by the bishop, offered them advice. " The God of the Christians," they said, " frequently helps those who cry to Him and His help is all powerful. Let us enquire whether He will be on our side and let us with a willing mind promise offerings that will be agreeable to Him." Accordingly, at their unanimous request, lots were cast and it was found that Christ was willing to help them. When this had been publicly notified, the hearts of all were forthwith so greatly encouraged that they wished to proceed immediately to make a bold attack on the town. "What," said they, " have we now to fear or dread? Christ is with us; let us fight and behave like men; nothing can withstand us, nor shall we fail to secure certain victory, for we have the mightiest of the gods as our helper. " When all were gathered together with courage and joy to attack the town, and they had invested it and were eager to commence the fight, those inside asked that an opportunity for speech be afforded them, and when the Swedish King had agreed, they immediately said, "We desire peace rather than fighting, and we wish to enter into an agreement with you. In the first place we are prepared to give you for the sake of securing an agreement all the gold and the arms that we took as spoil from the Danes last year. Furthermore, we offer half a pound of silver for each individual man now in this town, and in addition we will pay you the tribute which we formerly paid and will give hostages, for we desire henceforth to be subject and obedient to your rule, as we were in former time. When this offer had been made, the passions of the young men could not be assuaged, but being eager for action and devoid of fear, they desired only to fight and said that they would destroy by force of arms the town and all that the people possessed and would carry them off as captives. The king, however, and his chief men, were of a wiser opinion, and, having accepted their offer and entered into an agreement with them, they gladly returned home, taking with them countless treasures anti the thirty hostages that were provided. When at length peace had been established between the two peoples, the Swedes extolled with utmost zeal the omnipotence and glory of Christ our Lord and declared that He was greater than all other gods. They began also to ask with solicitude what they ought to give to him, by whom

THE LIFE OF ST. ANSGAR

they had obtained so great a victory. At the suggestion of some Christian merchants who were present at the time they promised that they would observe a fast that would be acceptable to the Lord Christ, and accordingly when they returned, after spending seven days at home they all abstained from eating flesh for another seven days. Moreover, when forty days had elapsed, they unanimously agreed to abstain from eating flesh for the forty days following. This was done, and all who were present carried out their resolve with willing minds. After this many in their reverence and love for Christ, began to lay stress upon the fasts observed by Christians and upon alms giving, and began to assist the poor because they had learnt that this was pleasing to Christ. Thus, with the goodwill of all did the priest Erimbert accomplish amongst them the things that pertained to God, and, whilst all applauded the power of Christ, the observance of the divine religion from that time forward increased in these parts and encountered opposition from no one.

CHAPTER XXXI.
Meanwhile [I.e. in 854] it happened by divine judgment that King Horic was killed in war in a disturbance caused by pirates whilst his relations were attempting to invade his kingdom. Together with him all the chief men of that land, who had formerly been acquaintances and friends of the bishop, perished by the sword. When at length the younger Horic had been established. in the kingdom, some of those who were then his chief men and had not been so well known to the bishop, tried to persuade him that the church that had. been built amongst them should be destroyed, and that the Christian religion should be abolished; for they said that their gods were angry and that these great evils had come upon them because they had accepted the worship of another and an unknown god. Accordingly, the headman of the village of Sliaswich, whose name was Hovi, who was specially opposed to this religion, urged the king to destroy the Christian faith, and he ordered the church that had been built there. to be shut and forbade the observance of the Christian religion. On this account the priest who was there retired thence, being forced to do so by the bitter persecution.

CHAPTER XXXII.

On this account the bishop was rendered very anxious and not a little sad because of the friends whom he had formerly attached to himself by generous gifts. There were none at the court of the younger Horic, by whose instrumentality he might win him to do what the Lord desired. Being then deprived of human aid, he hastened, as his custom was, to seek divine assistance. Nor did he fail to secure that for which he hoped, for the Lord strengthened him with spiritual consolation and he became assured that the religion which had begun to be established (in Sweden) would not perish, as the enemies of Christ were planning. With the help of the Lord matters turned out in the following way soon afterwards. When on this account he was arranging to go to the king, the Lord anticipated his action and the headman was expelled from the abovementioned village and had no prospect of being received back into favor, whereupon the king kindly sent his messenger to the bishop and asked him to send back his priest to his church. He at the same time declared that he, no less than the elder Horic, desired to deserve Christ's favor and to secure the friendship of the bishop. When then our venerable pastor came into the presence of the king, having as his helper the most noble Burghard, who had formerly assisted the elder Horic in all matters and had great influence with both kings because he was their relation, the king showed his pleasure in receiving him by permitting him immediately to do everything connected with the Christian religion which his predecessor had formerly allowed to be done. Moreover, he agreed that there should be a bell in the church, the use of which the pagans regarded as unlawful. In another village called Ripa, situated within his kingdom, he likewise gave a site for the erection of a church and granted permission for a priest to be there.

CHAPTER XXXIII.

While these things were being done the venerable Bishop Gautbert [At this time Bishop of Osnabrük] sent to the Swedes a priest called Ansfrid, who was of Danish descent and had been trained by Ebo for the service of the Lord. When he came thither, he and the priest Erimbert, who had returned thence, [I.e. in 854 or 855] continued there for three or four years and won the respect of all. But when he heard of the death of Gautbert, he returned, and having spent some time with us [I.e. in Bremen] was seized with sickness, and after suffering much pain he died. Whereupon the bishop, who would not allow the Christian faith which had arisen there to perish, arranged to send thither a priest named Ragenbert. He was specially fitted for this task and was most willing to undertake the journey, but while he was on his way to the port of Schleswig, where there were ships and merchants who were to make the journey with him, by the contrivance of the devil it happened that he was waylaid by Danish robbers and despoiled of all that he had, and on the Day of the Assumption of St. Mary he too, while endeavoring to carry out his good intentions, made a happy end. His death caused great distress to the bishop, but he could in no wise be hindered from carrying out his purpose, and soon afterwards he ordained for this work a priest named Rimbert, whose ancestors were of Danish extraction. When he had sent him in Christ's name to those parts he was kindly received there by the king and the people, and by the help of the Lord he celebrated without restraint the divine mysteries in their midst. To him, as to all the other priests whom he had before appointed to live among the pagans, Ansgar gave strict orders that they should not desire nor seek to obtain the property of anyone, but he affectionately exhorted them that after the example of the Apostle St. Paul [Cf. Acts xviii., 3] they should labor with their hands and be content with food and raiment. He, however, gave them and those who followed them in abundance out of his own possessions all that they wanted, and in addition whatever they needed to give away in order to secure friends.

CHAPTER XXXIV.

Furthermore, amid the many and varied difficulties which, as we have said, he endured in connection with this mission, although he was constantly strengthened by divine inspiration, which prevented him from abandoning the task that he had undertaken, the piety and spiritual fervor of Ebo the Archbishop of Rheims, who had first received the members of the mission, afforded him no little comfort. For Ebo, being inflamed with the desire to render effective the call of the non-Christian races, urged him to carry the blessings of the faith into those parts and impressed upon him that he should not abandon what he had begun. The good bishop, stirred by his exhortations and his enthusiasm on behalf of this cause, accomplished unhesitatingly the duties of the task that had been entrusted to him, nor could he be diverted from it by any trouble or inconvenience. Amongst the many words of advice and admonition uttered by the archbishop by which the bishop was gladdened and encouraged, he always remembered the last. conversation that they had when they conversed concerning this mission. When our bishop had enumerated the many troubles that had befallen him, and asked Ebo what he thought of the mission, and eagerly demanded whatever consolation he could offer, with a prophet's inspiration Ebo replied, "Be assured that what we have begun to do in the name of Christ, will bear fruit in the Lord. For it is my faith, and I firmly believe, nay I know of a truth, that although for the time being on account of our sins a hindrance may arise, the work that we have begun amongst these nations will never be entirely obliterated, but by the grace of God will bear fruit and prosper till the name of the Lord reach unto the ends of the earth." This too, was the faith of the others; with this purpose they set out to visit the distant nations; in their love for this religion, they strove on behalf of the Lord, from whom they will, without doubt, receive the reward of their toil. Such love and devotion were ever present in the mind of our lord and father, nor did he ever cease to pray for the salvation of these nations.

On the contrary, when the pirates, who came from the abovementioned nations, were continually attacking and the whole of his diocese was being devastated, and his household was being plundered, he nevertheless prayed earnestly for those who opposed and laid wait for him, and ceased not to entreat the mercy of God for those who illtreated him and to pray that their sin might not be reckoned to them, because, being ignorant of God's justice and being deceived by the devil, they had shown themselves the enemies of the Christian religion. His anxiety about their behalf was so keen that in his last illness, even till his last breath, he never failed to concern himself with and to plan on behalf of this mission. [Cf. Chap xli.] Possessed by this ardent zeal for religion he was taken from this mortal life, and we believe that on the resurrection day he will pass with honor and joy into the celestial kingdom accompanied by a great multitude of believers whom he had won for the Lord from amongst the Danes and Swedes and by the divine mercy will receive the reward for the good contest that he waged.

CHAPTER XXXV.

As we have now spoken at length concerning this mission and his anxiety to save others, the time has come to tell how he behaved himself with a view to the salvation of his own soul, and how in the fear of God he afflicted his body. There is no need to describe what you know well, the kind of life he led with you in the monastery, which was marked by abstinence and devotion. Nevertheless, he appeared - so we have heard to the elders and the aged to be wonderful and worthy of imitation. When he became a bishop amongst us he strove by every means to carry forward what he had begun in the monastery, and he specially endeavored to imitate the life of all the saints and of Martin in particular. For he wore sackcloth on his skin by night as well as by day, and in accordance with what he had read in Martin's life, he made a special effort to benefit the common people by preaching to them the word of God. At the same time, he loved to be alone in order that he might exercise himself in divine philosophy. With this end in view he had a special cell built for himself which he called a quiet place and one friendly to grief. Here he dwelt with a few companions and, as often as he could get free from preaching and ecclesiastical duties and the disturbances caused by the heathen, he dwelt here alone, but he never allowed his own convenience, or his love of solitude, to interfere with the interests of the flock that had been entrusted to him. Moreover, as long as he possessed any part of his youthful strength, he would often weigh out his bread and measure his water, and this more particularly as long as he was permitted to be alone. At this time, he was, as he himself stated greatly tempted by the spirit of ambition. For the enemy of the human race endeavored to corrupt his mind by this evil and he appeared great in his own eyes, because of his abstinence. On this account he was rendered sad and he turned to the Lord in prayer with all his might and prayed that His grace might set him free from this baleful impiety. And when for this reason he had given himself to earnest prayer and had fallen asleep one night, he beheld himself caught up to heaven and all the (inhabitants of the) world gathered into a dark valley, from which, albeit at rare intervals, the souls of the saints were caught up by angelic ministry and led into heaven. In this dark valley there was shown to him as it were the soil from which the human race had its origin. When he beheld all this with astonishment and horror, he was bidden to note the starting point of his present life and it was said to him, "How can a man boast who has had so base an origin in this valley of tears? And whatever good he possesses, has he not received it from Him from Whom comes every good gift and every perfect boon.'" [James I:17] "If therefore, "the voice said, " at any future time thou shalt be tempted by the pest of ambition, recall the origin of thy birth and by the grace of God thou shalt be set free." And thus, it happened. But after he grew old, he could not abstain from food in this way, but his drink continued to he water, though, for the sake of avoiding vainglory more than for the sake of taking anything pleasant, he was accustomed to mix wine with the small amount of water he was about to drink. And because in his old age he could not practice his accustomed abstinence, he endeavored to make up for this deficiency by almsgiving, prayers and other good deeds. For this reason, too he redeemed many captives whom he set free. [See chap viii] Some of these who were especially suitable he ordered to be given a religious education and to be trained for the service of God. Furthermore, the large manuscripts that are with us [I.e. in the monastery in Bremen] and which were copied out and marked by his own hand, witness to his zeal and his desire to intensify his devotion and love to God. These books are only known to include matters that belong to the glory of Almighty God, the refutation of sinners, the praise of eternal life, the terror of hell and whatever pertains to grief and lamentation. The brethren who are with you and those in New Corbey, whom he often asked to let him undertake this work and who sent him writings of this kind, are witnesses. But though he desired to pass his whole life in sorrow and tears he could never be satisfied. For although grief would often bring tears, he never considered this sufficient, though in the last year of his life by the goodness of the Lord he won the blessing which he had long sought of being able to shed tears as often as he desired. From the passages in Holy Scripture that relate to sorrow for sin and in the case of each separate psalm he would provide an appropriate prayer. This he was wont to call him pigmentum and in this way the psalms became sweet to him. And in these pigmenta he paid no attention to the arrangement of the words but sought only to attain sorrow of heart. In them at one time he praises the omnipotence and the judgment of God, at another time he upbraids and chides himself; at one time he lauds the saints who are obedient to God, at another time he mourns for those who are wretched and sinful. He was wont to say that he was himself worse than any of them. When others sung psalms with him the psalm came to an end he would meditate alone and in silence and would declare his meditations to no one. One of us who was a special friend [This probably refers to Rimbert] of his persuaded with difficulty and after much entreaty to dictate to him exactly that which he was wont to sing, but as long as he lived, he made known to no one what he had written, though after Ansgar's death he showed it to those who desired to read it. Whilst singing psalms he would frequently work with his hands, for at this time he was accustomed to make nets. In regard to the psalm., he arranged to sing some by night and some by day, some while he was preparing to sing Mass and some while he was returning with bare feet to his bed. In the morning while he was putting on his shoes and washing he would sing, a litany and when he went to church he would himself celebrate Mass three or four times, standing as he performed his office. At the usual appointed time he would sing the public Mass unless some difficulty intervened, and in this case, he would listen to the Mass. Who can declare how great was his liberality in the giving of alms, for he desired to make everything that he possessed minister, by the will of the Lord, to the needs of sufferers. Whenever he knew that anyone was in need he was concerned to aid to the utmost of his ability, and not only in his own diocese, but in distant regions he would provide help and assistance.

In particular he founded a hospital for the poor at Bremen, to which he assigned the tithes from certain hamlets so that those who were poor and sick might be daily sustained and refreshed. Throughout the whole of his episcopacy, he gave away for the support of the poor a tenth of the animals and of all his revenues and a tenth of the tithes which belonged to him, and whatever money or property of any kind came to him he gave a tenth for the benefit of the poor. In addition, every fifth year he tithed again all his animals although they had been already tithed in order to give alms. Of the money that came to the churches in the monasteries he gave a fourth part for this purpose. He was ever most careful of scholars and of widows and wherever he knew that there were hermits, whether men or women, he endeavored to visit them frequently and to strengthen them in God's service by gifts, and minister to their wants. He always carried in his girdle a little bag containing coins, so that, if anyone who was in need came and the dispenser of charity was not there, he might himself be able to give at once. For in all things, he strove to fulfil the saying of the blessed Job, that he would not even cause the eyes of the widow to wait. Thus did he endeavor to be an eye to the blind, and a foot to the lame and the father of the poor. He ordered that four indigent persons, two men and two women, should be received and fed daily at Bremen during Lent. He joined with the brethren in washing the feet of the men; in the case of the women this was done in the above-mentioned hospital for the poor by one who was consecrated to God and whom he had himself approved for her devotion to God and her love of religion. As he went round his parishes after the manner of a bishop, before he came to a meal, he ordered that some poor persons should be brought in, and he himself gave them water to wash their hands and blessed the food and drink and gave it to them. Then a table was placed in front of them and he and his guest began their own meal. We saw on one occasion an illustration of his compassion and piety which was afforded by the son of a certain widow who with many others had been carried as a captive to a distant land, that is to Sweden, and had been redeemed and brought back by him to his own country. When his mother was rejoicing at the sight of his return and as is the habit of women, was weeping for joy as she stood in his presence, the bishop, who was no less moved, begin to weep also. He then immediately restored to the widowed mother the son to whom he had given his freedom and suffered them to go home rejoicing.

CHAPTER XXXVI.

And inasmuch as, in accordance with the teaching of St. Paul, his conversation was always in heaven, he, though on earth, was frequently enlightened by celestial revelations, as we have already set forth, though with many omissions. Thus, it was that almost everything that was about to happen to him became known to him by a dream, or by mental enlightenment, or by an ecstatic vision. When we speak of mental enlightenment, we think that it resembled that referred to in the Acts of the Apostles [Acts viii. 29] where it is written, " The Spirit said to Philip. "For in the case of every important decision that he had to make he always desired to have time for consideration, and he decided nothing rashly till, being enlightened by God's grace, he knew what was best to be done. When he had thus obtained assurance by means of a heavenly vision he arranged everything that had to be done without hesitation. Moreover, in regard to the things which he beheld in dreams, as has already been frequently noted, they came true so often that we never remember a failure: in proof whereof let us refer to one instance that has not been mentioned. Before he was invited to take charge of the Church at Bremen, he bid a vision one night in which he appeared to have arrived at a most delightful place where he found the Apostle St. Peter. As he was gazing on him with astonishment certain men came who begged that he, St. Peter, would send them a teacher and pastor, and when he replied, "See here is the man whom you should have as your pastor," putting before them as he spoke the bishop who was standing before him, it seemed to him that there was a great earthquake and that he fell to the earth and that a voice above him spoke, and that he experienced a great mental happiness, even the unction of the Holy Spirit, so that he felt himself born again in the grace of Christ. The voice which came poured as it were a blessing upon him. Afterwards, as it seemed to him, the men before-mentioned urged the Apostle to send them a teacher, and he replied, as though he were displeased with them, " Did I not tell you that he should be your teacher who stands before you? Why do you doubt it? Did you not hear the voice of the Holy Spirit that came for this purpose, to consecrate a pastor for you?"

When he awoke from this dream which he had three years before he was invited to rule over the Church at Bremen, he was assured by what had been said that it was his duty to go somewhere in the Lord's name, but whither he knew not. When later on he came by order of the king to this church and learnt that it was consecrated in honor of St. Peter and found some there who would not willingly receive him, he remembered his vision, and because of it he agreed to undertake the charge of this diocese for, as he solemnly declared, he would not otherwise have been willing to do this. At the time when he had the abovementioned monastery at Turholt, and the calling of the heathen was his care, in order that he might be able to help them he caused some boys whom he had bought from the Northmen or Slavs to be brought up in the same monastery so that they might be trained for the holy warfare. When this monastery was given to Raginar he took some of these boys and sent them out as his servants, and on this account the bishop was specially distressed. In a vision which he had soon afterwards, he appeared to have come to a certain house and to have found there King Charles and Raginar. It seemed to him that he reproached them in regard to these boys and said that be had arranged to train them for the service of Almighty God and not to act as servants to Raginar. When he said this, it seemed to him that Raginar lifted his foot and kicked his mouth, and when this happened, he thought that the Lord Jesus Christ stood by him and said to the king and to Raginar, "To whom does this man whom ye treat so shamefully belong? Know that he has a Master and because of this you will not go unpunished." When he said this they were terrified and affrighted, whereupon the bishop awoke. The divine vengeance which overtook Raginar showed how true was the revelation. For a little later he incurred the displeasure of the king and lost the monastery and everything that he had received from the king, nor did he ever regain his former favor.

CHAPTER XXXVII.

We must not appear to pass over the quality and the extent of his pastoral service, for in him we have proof of what St. Gregory said concerning the pastors of the Church, when he was speaking figuratively of the shepherds who were watching over their flock when our Lord was born. " Why," said he, " did the angel appear to the watching shepherds, and why did God's light shine around them ? Was it not because they, above all others, deserve to behold the heavenly vision, who know how to superintend with care their faithful flocks? While they keep watch with pious care over their flock the divine grace shines ever more and more above them." In everything that he did God's grace was with him, as we have proved by many examples. For inasmuch as he was solicitous for the protection of his flock, he won the right to see heavenly visions and in many cases, as we have shown, his mind was inspired by the sight of things divine. Moreover, as the grace of God shone more and more in his body, his preaching had a special charm, though it was at times awe inspiring, so that it might be clearly seen that his words were controlled by divine inspiration. By mingling gentleness with terror he would make manifest the power of God's judgment, whereby the Lord when He comes will show Himself terrible to sinners and friendly to the just. His grace of speech and appearance were so attractive that he inspired with fear the powerful and rich and still more those who were impenitent and shameless, and whilst the common people embraced him as a brother, the poor with utmost affection venerated him as a father. Although he carefully avoided the signs of supernatural power as being an incentive to pride, nevertheless, though he sought it not, such signs were not wanting, and it was thereby manifestly proved that the commandment of the Lord that came forth from his mouth did not fail. For when on one occasion he was preaching to the people in the village of Ostarga in Frisia on the Lord's day, and in the course of his address was warning them not to do any manual work on a Feast Day, some who were obstinate and foolish, on their return home, seeing that the day was fine, went out into the meadow and collected hay into a heap. When this had been done and it drew towards evening, all the heaps that had been made on that day were destroyed by fire from heaven, whilst those remained uninjured which stood in the midst of the meadow and had been made on the previous days. Thereupon the people who dwelt round, when they saw the smoke from a distance, thought that an enemy was approaching and were greatly afraid, but when they had made careful enquiry into the facts they assured themselves that obstinacy had received its punishment.

CHAPTER XXXVIII.

We ought not to pass over in silence the fact that the Northalbingians on one occasion committed a great crime and one of a terrible nature. When some unhappy captives, who had been taken from Christian lands and carried away to the barbarians, were ill-treated by these strangers, they fled thence in the hope of escaping and came to the Christians, that is to the Northalbingians who, as is well known, live next to the pagans, but when they arrived these Christians showed no compassion but seized them and bound them with chains. Some of them they sold to pagans, whilst others they enslaved, or sold to other Christians. When the bishop heard this, he was greatly distressed that so great a crime had been perpetrated in his diocese, but he could not devise how he might mend matters because there were many involved who were esteemed to be powerful and noble. When he was much distressed on this account there was granted to him one night the customary consolation. For it seemed to him that the Lord Jesus was in this world, as He had once been, when He gave to men His teaching and example. It seemed to him that He went with a multitude of the faithful and that he, the bishop, was with Him on His journey, glad and rejoicing because there was no opposition, but a divinely infused fear was upon the arrogant, and the oppressors were removed and a great quiet prevailed, so that there appeared to be no contradiction or opposition on the journey. Having seen this vision, he prepared to go to this people with the desire by some means or other to set free the unhappy men who had been sold and given over to an outrageous servitude and by the Lord's help to prevent anyone from committing hereafter so great a crime. On this journey the Lord so greatly assisted him and caused the fear of his power so to overawe those who were arrogant that, though these men were of rank and exercised harmful influence, none of them ventured to oppose his advice or resist his authority, but the unhappy men were sought out wherever they had been sold and were given their liberty and allowed to go wherever they desired. Furthermore, in order to prevent any deceit being practiced thereafter they made an agreement that none of those who had defiled themselves by the seizure of these captives should defend himself, either by taking an oath or by producing witnesses, but should commend himself to the judgment of Almighty God, whether it was the man who was accused of the crime or the captive who accused him. Thus did the Lord manifest on this journey the truth of the promise which He made to those who believe when He said, " Lo I am with you all the days even unto the end of the world." [Matt xxviii., 20] So prosperously and joyfully did he accomplish this journey that those who were with him said that never in his life did he have such a good and pleasant journey, for they said, " Now of the truth we know that the Lord was with us."

CHAPTER XXXIX.

It is impossible to count the number of those who were healed by his prayers and by his anointing. For, according to the statement made by many persons, sick people came eagerly to him, not only from his own diocese, but from a great distance, demanding from him healing medicine. He, however, preferred that this should be kept quiet rather than that it should be noised abroad. For when these signs of power were spoken of on one occasion in his presence, he said to a friend, " Were I worthy of such a favor from my God, 1 would ask that he would grant to me this one miracle, that by His grace He would make of me a good man."

CHAPTER XL.

The life that he lived involved toils which were accompanied by constant bodily suffering: In fact his whole life was like martyrdom. He endured many labors amongst foreigners apart from those within his own diocese, which were caused by the invasions and ravages of barbarians and the opposition of evil men, and in addition the personal suffering which, for the love of Christ, he never ceased to bring upon himself. But what can we do when, after mentioning so many things that were pleasant and profitable, we are compelled to mention which it is impossible for us to explain without sorrow? For in the sixty-fourth year of his age [I.e. In 864], which was the thirtyfourth year of his episcopate, he began to suffer from a serious illness, namely dysentery. When after many days, that is four months, or even more, he was still in pain and felt that he was nigh unto death, he continued to give God thanks and said that his pain was less than his sins deserved, and he would often repeat the words of Job " If we have received good at the Lord's hand, why should we not endure evil?" [Job II.,10] Nevertheless, he became very sad, because as a result of his visions he had believed that he would die by martyrdom rather than by an illness of this kind, and he began to reflect upon his sins, because by his own fault he had been deprived of what seemed to him a certain anticipation, and he would often repeat the words of the psalmist, " Thou are just, O Lord, and thy judgment is righteous." Ps. cxix., 137] He would make known this grief to his most trusty disciple [This almost certainly refers to Rimbert, the author of this biography] who shared with him his sorrows, and who would strive earnestly to comfort him by telling him that it had not been promised that he should be slain with the sword, or burnt in the fire, or killed by water, but that he should come into the presence of the Lord wearing a crown of martyrdom. Ansgar, however, could receive no such consolation. He would often converse with his disciple concerning this matter, who in his eager desire to bring comfort tried to remind him of all that he had suffered in God's service and how much bodily pain he had endured: he urged, moreover, that, even if he had suffered none of these things, his last grievous illness, which had continued day after day, would by God's grace more than have earned for him the title of martyr. He would, however, receive no consolation of this kind but continued to grieve, and thus it came about that the Lord deigned to comfort his servant tint, as formerly, by a dream but by an open revelation, in order that for so great a grief he might provide a surpassing remedy. For one day when he was standing in the Oratory at the Mass and was greatly distressed on this account, he experienced a sudden ecstasy and heard a voice which chided him earnestly because he had doubted God's promise and had thought that any evildoing could be mightier than God's goodness. The voice said, " Believe firmly and in no wise doubt that God of His grace will grant both favors, that is, H will forgive the sins concerning which you are anxious and will accomplish all that He promised. Having received this consolation he was comforted.

CHAPTER XLI.

After this he began to arrange with special care the matters that needed attention in his diocese. Moreover, he gave orders that the privileges granted by the apostolic see which concerned his mission, should be set forth in a number of copies and should be distributed amongst nearly all the bishops in

Ludovic's kingdom. To Ludovic himself and to his son who bore the same name he sent a copy and added letters bearing his own name in which he begged that they would remember these matters and give help as circumstances might dictate, in order that, by the help of God and their assistance, the mission among the pagan races might bear fruit and develop. When then he had suffered from his sickness continuously for three months and the season of Epiphany had gone, be desired that he might be permitted to pass into the Lord's favor [The Codex Ambianensis reads gloriam.] on the feast of the Purification of St. Mary. And as this festival drew near he commanded that an entertainment should be prepared for the clergy and the poor so that they might feast on this most sacred day. He commanded also that three tapers should be made from his special wax, which he regarded as specially good.

When these had been made he had them carried in front of him on the vigil of this festival [I.e. on February 1st]. When they were brought, he ordered that one should be placed in front of the altar of St. Mary, another in front of the altar of St. Peter, and a third in front of the altar of St. John the Baptist, as he hoped that those who in his vision [see chap iii] had been his guides would receive him when he departed from the body. But he was so wearied and worn out by his sickness that hardly anything of him was left in the body except his bones which were bound together with sinews and covered with skin. Nevertheless, he continued constantly to praise the Lord, and when the day of this festival dawned nearly all the priests who were present celebrated Masses on his behalf, as had been their daily custom. He proceeded to arrange the nature of the discourse that was to be made to the people and declared that on this day he would not taste anything until the public Mass was finished. When it was finished and he had eaten and drunken in moderation he spent nearly the whole day in giving counsel to his companions and in enkindling their devotion, inciting them as far as he was able, at one time as a community and at another time as individuals, to serve God. He was, however, most anxious and solicitous concerning his own mission to the heathen. He spent also the following night in giving advice of this kind. He asked the brethren who were present when they had said the litany and sung the psalms in view of his departing, in accordance with their custom, to sing together the Te Deum and the catholic creed, composed by St. Athanasius. When the morning came and almost all the priests who were present had celebrated Mass on his behalf and he had received the communion of the body and blood of the Lord, he lifted up his hand and prayed that God in His goodness would forgive whoever had done him any wrong. Then he began to say over and over again the verses, " According to Thy mercy think thou upon me, according to Thy goodness, O Lord," [Ps xxv., 6] and " God be merciful to me a sinner," [Luke xviii., 18] and " Into

Thy hands, O Lord, I commend my spirit.". [Luke xxiii., 46, Ps xxxi.,6] And when he had said these words many times and could not continue through lack of breath, he ordered one of the brethren [I.e. Rimbert: Cf. *Vita Rimberti* chap ix] to continue saying the same words in his behalf, and so, with his eyes fixed on heaven, he breathed forth his spirit which had been commended to the grace of the Lord.

When his body had been treated in the customary manner it was placed upon a bier and taken to the church, as was done in the case of St. Martin, [Cf chap xxxv., note] amidst the lamentations of all and the unanimous mourning of clergy, orphans, widows, scholars and the poor.

CHAPTER XLII.

Although no doubt could arise in regard to his salvation, what monk or other believer could refrain from weeping, in view of the fact that he, in whom the lives of nearly all the saints of early times were reproduced, had left us desolate. To go back to the Head of all God's elect, he as a poor man followed Christ who was also poor; like the apostles he abandoned all that he possessed, and like St. john the Baptist he sought out the solitude of a monastery and lived his early life far removed from the coming and going of men. [Luke I.80] When, in course of time, he had gradually grown up and had advanced from one virtue to another, he who was destined to become a chosen vessel in order, like the apostle St. Paul, to bear Christ's name to the heathen nations, [Acts ix.15] afterwards, like St. Peter the chief of the apostles, undertook the charge of feeding Christ's sheep. [John xxi.17] As a ruler he displayed such qualities and such greatness that as can be abundantly proved he acted as a mediator between heaven and earth, and between God and his neighbor, and whilst on some occasions he enjoyed heavenly visions and celestial revelations, at other times he guided the life and actions of those entrusted to his care. The two wings of the active and the contemplative life he himself completely possessed, for whilst, according to the teaching of the gospels, the pure in heart shall see God, [Matt v.8] he, who in his virgin purity was chosen by God, continued throughout his life, like St. John the apostle and evangelist, as a virgin both in mind and body. He was, moreover, possessed by so great love towards all men that like the first martyr St. Stephen he prayed even for his enemies, [Acts vii.59] How blessed was he and worthy of all praise and commendation, who imitated the greatest of the saints, and was endowed with unnumbered virtues, who, being holy in mind and chaste in body, shall, with the virgins, follow the Lamb whithersoever He goes, [Rev xiv.4] and, who continuing ever as a confessor of Christ, shall have a glorious place amidst His confessors and in the regeneration shall sit with the apostles on their lofty seat of judgment, to judge the world which he had despised and to receive with the martyrs the crown of justice and the divinely promised palm of martyrdom. For it is clear that there are two kinds of martyrdom, one which occurs when the Church is at peace, and which is hidden from sight ; the other which occurs in a time of persecution and is visible to all. He desired both kinds of martyrdom, but one only did he attain. For day by day, by tears, watchings, fastings, tormenting of the flesh and mortification of his carnal desires, he offered up a sacrifice to God on the altar of his heart and attained to martyrdom as far as was possible in a time of peace. And inasmuch as the agent, though not the will, was lacking in order to bring about the visible martyrdom of the body, he obtained in will what he could not obtain in fact. We cannot, however, altogether deny that he attained actual martyrdom if we compare his great labors with those of the apostle. In journeyings often, in perils of waters, in perils of robbers, in perils from his own race, in perils from the heathen, in perils in the city, in perils in lonely places, in perils in the sea, in perils among false brethren ; in labor and distress, in watchings often, in hunger and thirst, in fastings; often, in cold and nakedness ; besides those things which are without, that which came upon him daily, the care of all the Churches. Who was weak and he was not? Who, was offended and he did not burn? [Cf. II Cor xi.26-29]

How then, shall he, who, for the Lord's sake, was vexed by such great bodily troubles and mental disquietude, be denied the title of martyr? For if only a life that ends in suffering can be regarded as that of a martyr, then to no purpose did the Lord declare that the evangelist St. John, whose life, as we know, did not end in martyrdom, should drink of His cup. [Matt xx.23] If then we do not doubt that, in accordance with the statement of the Lord, St. John is to be reckoned amongst the martyrs, we ought to have no hesitation regarding this holy and blessed man who has gone before us. For he was indeed a martyr, because, according to the apostle, the world was crucified to him and he to the world. [Gal vi.14] He was a martyr because, amid the temptations of the devil, the enticements of the flesh, the persecutions of the heathen and the opposition of Christians, he continued to the end of his life unperturbed, immovable, and unconquerable as a confessor of Christ. He was a martyr, for, whilst the word martyr [I.e. the Greek word "martyr"] signifies witness, he was a witness of God's word and of the Christian name. Wherefore let no one be surprised that he did not attain to that martyrdom which he so greatly desired and which, he thought, had been promised to him, [See chaps. iii and xl] for it cannot be proved that this was promised as he himself interpreted the word martyrdom. In the case of visible martyrdom pride might affect the mind. In order to avoid this, God, in His providence, promised and granted that, his merits should suffer no diminution, while his humility, which is the guardian of all the virtues, should be preserved. Wherefore, inasmuch as it is clear from what we have above narrated how remarkable was his holiness and how great were his merits in God's sight, it remains that, as he was in all things an imitator of Christ, we too should strive to be imitators of him. So too will it become possible that he may live with us on earth to the end of the world, and we may be worthy to live with him in heaven after our present life is ended. For he will live with us on earth, if the holiness of his life and the remembrance of his teaching recall him to us. We too shall live with him in heaven if we follow his example, if with all our strength and desire we long for Him to Whom he has gone before us, Jesus Christ our Lord, Who with the Father and the Holy Spirit liveth and reigneth for ever and ever. *Amen.*

HYMNS

This hymn occurs in the Breviary used in the Swedish Church at Upsala.

Ansgari, pater optime,
Errantes nos in devio,
Reduc tuo juvamine
Servans sub Christi gremio.
Danis et Suecis gratiae
Donum fidemque praedicas
Pugil fortis in acie
Gentes Deo sanctificas.
Notam facis incredulis,
Doctrinan evangelicam,
Lucem ministrans populis
Ducis in viam coelicam.
Bonus pastor viriliter
Gregern pascis dominicum,
Informans, quod veraciter
Christuin colat magnificum.
Prudens talenta gratiae
Cum lucri magnitudine
Adduces regi gloriae
In pacis pulchritudine.
Deo patri sit gloria
Ejusque soli Filio,
Cum spiritu Paraclito
In sempiterna saecula.

The following represents an attempt to reproduce the original metre.

Most noble father, Ansgar,
Restore us by thy grace,
And those who wander now afar
In Christ's own bosom place.
In holy strife contending
Thou did'st the faith proclaim
To Danes and Swedes declaring
The honour of His name.
An unbelieving nation
From thee the light receives,
The teachings of salvation,
It now with joy believes.
Thou to God's sheep hast given
The food they fain would claim,

And earnestly hast striven
To glorify His name.
To the great King thou bringest
When earthly strife doth cease,
The talents thou receivest,
With manifold increase.
To Father, and His only Son
Be laud and honour given
To Holy Spirit, Three in One
In earth and highest heaven.

This hymn in honour of Anshar was written by Conrad Benne, who was a deacon in the monastery of S.S. Willehad and Stephen at Bremen from 1429 to 1456. It is included in the Missal of the Church at Bremen issued by Archbishop Johann Rode.

Jocundare plebs Bremensis
de tam miris et inimensis
donis tibi hic ostensis
cum decore vario.
Laeta tono psalle cano
glorioso de patrono
triumphante summo throno
beato Anschario.
Forma vitae Romanorum,
pontifex Nordalbingorum
arce tenet in polorum
mercedem negocio.
Antris sub Corbejae fotus,
cunctis sanctitate notus,
sic ad surnmum fit promotus
gradum sacerdotium.
Dispensator hic fidelis
Danos adit tensis velis
agnum dominantern caelis
terrae pandit finibus.
Corda sicca barbarorum
dulci de eloquiorum
fonte rigans divinorum
signis et virtutibus.
Victor trium fit regnorum,
fana stravit prophanorum,
cultu vano idoloyum
facto prorsus exulem.

Fide fulgent gens
Danorum,
Sueonumque, Norveborum,
Grandlanddeum, Islandorum
sub Bremensi praesule.
O mens tendens ad superna,
o sal terre, o lucerna,
luce splendens sempiterna,
latens non sub modio.
Flet antistes in agone,
se frustrari spe coronae,
reproinissa visione,
spirans pro inartyrio.
Calice de passionis
bibit veri Salomonis
licet citra vim mucronis
mortis cruciamina.
Inter probra tot tortorum,
fremitus tot tyrannorum,
fidei persecutorum,
vitae tot discrimina.
Speculandi spe quietis
cellam struit in rubetis,
pasturn poturn ceres thetis,
cui dat libamina.
Nunc in ymis operatur,
nunc in summis contemplatur,
duplex ita colebatur
vita sacro flamine.
Cum triumphi gades fixit
Christo, cui totus vixit,
hunc commendo tibi, dixit,
Jesu bone, spiriturn.
Corde sursum elevato,
fratribus vale dato,
raptu rapitur beato,
caeli ad exercitum.
O Anschari, pater pie,
venerantur te hoc die,
esto ductor hujus vitae
virtutum in gressibus.
In hac valle peregrina,
gregem ad ovile mina,

ne errantem faux lupina
saevis voret morsibus.

The translation follows:

Ye men of Bremen sing with joy,
Your hearts wid minds and tongues employ,
Such wondrous gifts without alloy
Each with beauty all its own
Of joyful sound the piercing reed
To praise your glorious patron, speed.
Blest Ansgar, now from troubles freed
High on his triumphal throne.
He, God's High priest midst Northmen rude
The pattern life to Romans shewed
In Heaven's high fortress unsubdued
Now holds his prize in glory.
Once nurtured up in Corbey's Hall,
His sanctity acclaimed by all,
To highest priesthood hears his call,
Rejoice, and sing his story.
With wide stretched sails, in faith he flies
Displays to wondering Danish eyes
The Lamb of God that rules the skies,
Bids them worship at His Shrine.
In pagan lands hard hearts he breaks,
Disciples for the Mister makes
Thy signs and merits conscience wakes,
Fount of eloquence divine!
The conqueror of kingdoms three,
Temples profane destroyed must be
Vain idol worship fain must flee,
For Christ are won these regions
In faith shine forth the Danes and Swedes
Where Bremen's faithful bishop leads
Icelanders, too, forsake their creeds
Greenlanders and Norwegians.
Oh I mind upraised, to things on high
Oh I salt of earth! oh sanctity !
Oh I light, no bushel hidden by,
Shining now with heavenly beam !
The warrior weeps, with grief cast down
Lest he should lose the martyr's crown,

THE LIFE OF ST. ANSGAR

'Twas surely promised for his own,
Once in brightest vision's gleam.
The Cup of Solomon the True [*ie. The messiah, David's greatest son*]
He drinketh yea, death's tortures too,
Though not by violent sword thrust through
Martrrdom he is denied.
Abuse and threats on every hand,
Tormentors, tyrants, round him stand,
His life a sign to every land
Faith triumphant will abide.
In hope of coiaemplation sweet
In thickest forest finds retreat
And there pours out oblation meet,
Corn and wine in Jesus name.
For though absorbed in cares of earth
He loves the things of highest worth
Two lives he leads; e'en from his birth
Brightly burns the sacred flame.
To Christ, of all his life the End
Triumphantly his steps do bend,
"To Thee my spirit I cornmend,
Dear Lord," he breathes, believing
Then to his brethren bids farewell,
Is taken up, in heaven to dwell
With raptureThose who loved him well
Can scarce refrain their grieving.
Oh! Ansgar blest, to thee we pray
As we revere thy name today,
Be thou our leader that we may
The path of virtue cherish.
Guide ever through the trackless world
Thy pilgrim sheep to the true fold,
Lest wolves upon thy flock take hold
And far from home we perish.

The Scriptorium Project is the work of a small group of lay people of various apostolic churches who are interested in the preservation, transmission, and translation of the works of the early and medieval church. Our efforts are to make the works of the church fathers accessible to anyone who might have an interest in Christian antiquities and the theological, philosophical, and moral writings that have become the bedrock of Western Civilization.

To-date, our releases have pulled from the Greek, Syriac, Georgian, Latin, Armenian, Slavic, Gothic, Nordic, Celtic, Ethiopian, and Coptic traditions of Christianity, and have been pulled from sundry local traditions and languages.

Other Titles from the Nordic Church (Norway, Sweden, Denmark):

Of the Highest Good by Boethius of Dacia (Dec. 2007)
Privileges & Oaths by Magnus VI, King of Norway (Apr. 2008)
Non Parum Animus Noster by Pope Alexander III (May 2008)
Revelations- Book I by St. Bridget of Sweden (June 2008)
The Life of St. Ansgar by Rimbert of Hamburg (July 2008)
The Eternity of the World by Boethius of Dacia (Aug. 2008)
Letter on the Institutes of the Law by Magnus VI, King of Norway (Nov. 2023)
Letters from the North: Catholic Missionaries in Scandinavia (Dec. 2023)

www.ingramcontent.com/pod-product-compliance
Lightning Source LLC
LaVergne TN
LVHW061041070526
838201LV00073B/5137